Optimizing Databricks Workloads

Harness the power of Apache Spark in Azure and maximize the performance of modern big data workloads

Anirudh Kala

Anshul Bhatnagar

Sarthak Sarbahi

BIRMINGHAM—MUMBAI

Optimizing Databricks Workloads

Publishing Product Manager: Dhruv Jagdish Kataria
Senior Editor: David Sugarman
Content Development Editor: Priyanka Soam
Technical Editor: Sonam Pandey
Copy Editor: Safis Editing
Project Coordinator: Aparna Ravikumar Nair
Proofreader: Safis Editing
Indexer: Subalakshmi Govindhan
Production Designer: Aparna Bhagat

First published: December 2021

Production reference: 1171121

Published by Packt Publishing Ltd.
Livery Place
35 Livery Street
Birmingham
B3 2PB, UK.

ISBN 978-1-80181-907-7

www.packt.com

Mr. Rajesh Sarbahi
31st October 1964 – 12th April 2021

I, Sarthak, dedicate this book to my dear father, who motivated and inspired me to work hard and lead a life I could be proud of one day. He taught me to face challenges and live a truly wealthy life. The love and support will always be there with all those wonderful memories in our hearts.
We miss you, dad.

Contributors

About the authors

Anirudh Kala is an expert in machine learning techniques, artificial intelligence, and natural language processing. He has helped multiple organizations to run their large-scale data warehouses with quantitative research, natural language generation, data science exploration, and big data implementation. He has worked in every aspect of data analytics using the Azure data platform. Currently, he works as the director of Celebal Technologies, a data science boutique firm dedicated to large-scale analytics. Anirudh holds a computer engineering degree from the University of Rajasthan and his work history features the likes of IBM and ZS Associates.

Anshul Bhatnagar is an experienced, hands-on data architect involved in the architecture, design, and implementation of data platform architectures, and distributed systems. He has worked in the IT industry since 2015 in a range of roles such as Hadoop/Spark developer, data engineer, and data architect. He has also worked in many other sectors including energy, media, telecoms, and e-commerce. He is currently working for a data and AI boutique company, Celebal Technologies, in India. He is always keen to hear about new ideas and technologies in the areas of big data and AI, so look him up on LinkedIn to ask questions or just to say hi.

Sarthak Sarbahi is a certified data engineer and analyst with a wide technical breadth and a deep understanding of Databricks. His background has led him to a variety of cloud data services with an eye toward data warehousing, big data analytics, robust data engineering, data science, and business intelligence. Sarthak graduated with a degree in mechanical engineering.

About the reviewer

Sawyer Nyquist is a consultant based in Grand Rapids, Michigan, USA. His work focuses on business intelligence, data analytics engineering, and data platform architecture. He holds these certifications from Microsoft: MCSA BI Reporting, Data Analyst Associate, and Azure Data Engineer Associate; and holds the Associate Developer certification for Apache Spark 3.0. Over his career, he worked with dozens of companies to strategize and implement data, analytics, and technology to drive growth. He is passionate about delivering enterprise data analytics solutions by building ETL pipelines, designing SQL data warehouses, and deploying modern cloud technologies for custom dashboards and reporting. He currently works as a senior consultant at Microsoft.

Table of Contents

3

Learning about Machine Learning and Graph Processing in Databricks

Section 2: Optimization Techniques

4

Managing Spark Clusters

5

Big Data Analytics

6

Databricks Delta Lake

7

Spark Core

Section 3: Real-World Scenarios

8
Case Studies

Other Books You May Enjoy

Index

Preface

Databricks is an industry-leading, cloud-based platform for data analytics, data science, and data engineering supporting thousands of organizations across the world in their data journey. It is a fast, easy, and collaborative Apache Spark-based big data analytics platform for data science and data engineering in the cloud.

In *Optimizing Databricks Workloads*, you will get started with a brief introduction to Azure Databricks and quickly begin to understand the important optimization techniques. The book covers how to select the optimal Spark cluster configuration for running big data processing and workloads in Databricks, some very useful optimization techniques for Spark DataFrames, best practices for optimizing Delta Lake, and techniques to optimize Spark jobs through Spark core. It contains an opportunity to learn about some of the real-world scenarios where optimizing workloads in Databricks has helped organizations increase performance and save costs across various domains.

By the end of this book, you will be prepared with the necessary toolkit to speed up your Spark jobs and process your data more efficiently.

Who this book is for

This book is for data engineers, data scientists, and cloud architects who have working knowledge of Spark/Databricks and some basic understanding of data engineering principles. Readers will need to have a working knowledge of Python, and some experience of SQL in PySpark and Spark SQL is beneficial.

What this book covers

Chapter 1, Discovering Databricks, will help you learn the fundamentals of Spark and all the different features of the Databricks platform and workspace.

Chapter 2, Batch and Real-Time Processing in Databricks, will help you learn about the SQL/DataFrame API for processing batch loads and the Streaming API for processing real-time data streams.

Chapter 3, Learning about Machine Learning and Graph Processing in Databricks, will help you get an introduction to machine learning on big data using SparkML and the Spark Graph Processing API.

Chapter 4, Managing Spark Clusters, will help you learn to select the optimal Spark cluster configurations for running big data processing and workloads in Databricks.

Chapter 5, Big Data Analytics, will help you learn some very useful optimization techniques for Spark DataFrames.

Chapter 6, Databricks Delta Lake, will help you learn the best practices for optimizing Delta Lake workloads in Databricks.

Chapter 7, Spark Core, will help you learn techniques to optimize Spark jobs through a true understanding of Spark core.

Chapter 8, Case Studies, will look at a number of real-world case studies where Databricks played a crucial role in an organization's data journey. We will also learn how Databricks is helping drive innovation across various industries around the world.

To get the most out of this book

In this book, we will be learning extensively about Azure Databricks. Being a cloud-native platform, Databricks can be accessed by any modern-day web browsing software, such as Google Chrome, Safari, Mozilla Firefox, or Microsoft Edge.

Software/hardware covered in the book	Operating system requirements
Azure Databricks (Chrome, Firefox, Edge, or Safari)	Windows, macOS, or Linux

If you are using the digital version of this book, we advise you to type the code yourself or access the code from the book's GitHub repository (a link is available in the next section). Doing so will help you avoid any potential errors related to the copying and pasting of code.

Download the example code files

You can download the example code files for this book from GitHub at `https://github.com/PacktPublishing/Optimizing-Databricks-Workload`. If there's an update to the code, it will be updated in the GitHub repository.

We also have other code bundles from our rich catalog of books and videos available at `https://github.com/PacktPublishing/`. Check them out!

Download the color images

We also provide a PDF file that has color images of the screenshots and diagrams used in this book. You can download it here: `https://static.packt-cdn.com/downloads/9781801819077_ColorImages.pdf`.

Conventions used

There are a number of text conventions used throughout this book.

`Code in text`: Indicates code words in text, database table names, folder names, filenames, file extensions, pathnames, dummy URLs, user input, and Twitter handles. Here is an example: "The preceding code block creates a Spark DataFrame and displays the first 1,000 records. Now, let's run some code with the `collect()` function."

A block of code is set as follows:

```
airlines_1987_to_2008.select('Year').distinct().collect()
```

Bold: Indicates a new term, an important word, or words that you see onscreen. For instance, words in menus or dialog boxes appear in **bold**. Here is an example: "Click on **Spark Jobs** under this command and select **View** next to the second job. This opens up the job page in Spark UI."

> **Tips or Important Notes**
> Executor slots are also called **cores** or **threads**.

Get in touch

Feedback from our readers is always welcome.

General feedback: If you have questions about any aspect of this book, email us at `customercare@packtpub.com` and mention the book title in the subject of your message.

Errata: Although we have taken every care to ensure the accuracy of our content, mistakes do happen. If you have found a mistake in this book, we would be grateful if you would report this to us. Please visit `www.packtpub.com/support/errata` and fill in the form.

Piracy: If you come across any illegal copies of our works in any form on the internet, we would be grateful if you would provide us with the location address or website name. Please contact us at `copyright@packt.com` with a link to the material.

If you are interested in becoming an author: If there is a topic that you have expertise in and you are interested in either writing or contributing to a book, please visit `authors.packtpub.com`.

Share Your Thoughts

Once you've read *Optimizing Databricks Workloads*, we'd love to hear your thoughts! Scan the QR code below to go straight to the Amazon review page for this book and share your feedback.

https://packt.link/r/1-801-81907-6

Your review is important to us and the tech community and will help us make sure we're delivering excellent quality content.

Section 1: Introduction to Azure Databricks

In this section, we cover a quick introduction to Azure Databricks and several of its APIs for analyzing and processing big data – DataFrames, ML, Graph, and Streaming.

This section comprises the following chapters:

- *Chapter 1, Discovering Databricks*
- *Chapter 2, Batch and Real-Time Processing in Databricks*
- *Chapter 3, Learning about Machine Learning and Graph Processing in Databricks*

1
Discovering Databricks

The original creators of **Apache Spark** established **Databricks** to solve the world's toughest data problems. Databricks was launched as a Spark-based unified data analytics platform in the cloud.

In this chapter, we will begin by understanding the internal architecture of Apache Spark™. This will be followed by an introduction to the basic components of Databricks. The following topics will be covered in this chapter:

- Introducing Spark fundamentals
- Introducing Databricks
- Learning about Delta Lake

Technical requirements

For this chapter, you will need the following:

- An Azure subscription
- Azure Databricks

Please refer to the code sample from: Code samples from `https://github.com/ PacktPublishing/Optimizing-Databricks-Workload/tree/main/ Chapter01`

Introducing Spark fundamentals

Spark is a distributed data processing framework capable of analyzing large datasets. At its very core, it consists of the following:

- **DataFrames**: Fundamental data structures consisting of rows and columns.
- **Machine Learning** (**ML**): Spark ML provides ML algorithms for processing big data.
- **Graph processing**: GraphX helps to analyze relationships between objects.
- **Streaming**: Spark's Structured Streaming helps to process real-time data.
- **Spark SQL**: A SQL to Spark engine with query plans and a cost-based optimizer.

DataFrames in Spark are built on top of **Resilient Distributed Datasets** (**RDDs**), which are now treated as the assembly language of the Spark ecosystem. Spark is compatible with various programming languages – Scala, Python, R, Java, and SQL.

Spark encompasses an architecture with one driver node and multiple worker nodes. The driver and worker nodes together constitute a **Spark cluster**. Under the hood, these nodes are based in **Java Virtual Machines** (**JVMs**). The driver is responsible for assigning and coordinating work between the workers.

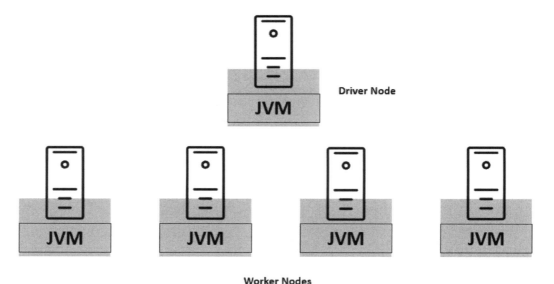

Figure 1.1 – Spark architecture – driver and workers

The worker nodes have **executors** running inside each of them, which host the Spark program. Each executor consists of one or more **slots** that act as the compute resource. Each slot can process a single unit of work at a time.

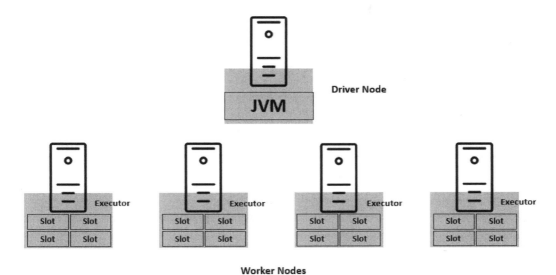

Figure 1.2 – Spark architecture – executors and slots

Every executor reserves memory for two purposes:

- Cache
- Computation

The cache section of the memory is used to store the DataFrames in a compressed format (called caching), while the compute section is utilized for data processing (aggregations, joins, and so on). For resource allocation, Spark can be used with a cluster manager that is responsible for provisioning the nodes of the cluster. Databricks has an in-built cluster manager as part of its overall offering.

> **Note**
> Executor slots are also called **cores** or **threads**.

Spark supports parallelism in two ways:

- **Vertical parallelism**: Scaling the number of slots in the executors
- **Horizontal parallelism**: Scaling the number of executors in a Spark cluster

Spark processes the data by breaking it down into chunks called **partitions**. These partitions are usually 128 MB blocks that are read by the executors and assigned to them by the driver. The size and the number of partitions are decided by the driver node. While writing Spark code, we come across two functionalities, **transformations** and **actions**. Transformations instruct the Spark cluster to perform changes to the DataFrame. These are further categorized into **narrow transformations** and **wide transformations**. Wide transformations lead to the shuffling of data as data requires movement across executors, whereas narrow transformations do not lead to re-partitioning across executors.

Running these transformations does not make the Spark cluster do anything. It is only when an action is called that the Spark cluster begins execution, hence the saying *Spark is lazy*. Before executing an action, all that Spark does is make a data processing plan. We call this plan the **Directed Acyclic Graph** (**DAG**). The DAG consists of various transformations such as read, filter, and join and is triggered by an action.

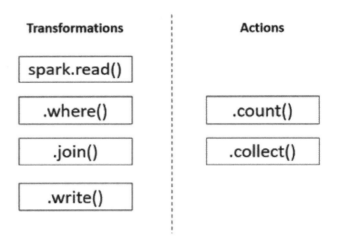

Figure 1.3 – Transformations and actions

Every time a DAG is triggered by an action, a **Spark job** gets created. A Spark job is further broken down into **stages**. The number of stages depends on the number of times a shuffle occurs. All narrow transformations occur in one stage while wide transformations lead to the formation of new stages. Each stage comprises of one or more **tasks** and each task processes one partition of data in the slots. For wide transformations, the stage execution time is determined by its slowest running task. This is not the case with narrow transformations.

At any moment, one or more tasks run parallelly across the cluster. Every time a Spark cluster is set up, it leads to the creation of a **Spark session**. This Spark session provides entry into the Spark program and is accessible with the spark keyword.

Sometimes, a few tasks process small partitions while others process larger chunks, we call this **data skewing**. This skewing of data should always be avoided if you hope to run efficient Spark jobs. In a broad execution, the stage is determined by its slowest task, so if a task is slow, the overall stage is slow and everything waits for that to finish. Also, whenever a wide transformation is run, the number of partitions of the data in the cluster changes to 200. This is a default setting, but can be modified using Spark configuration.

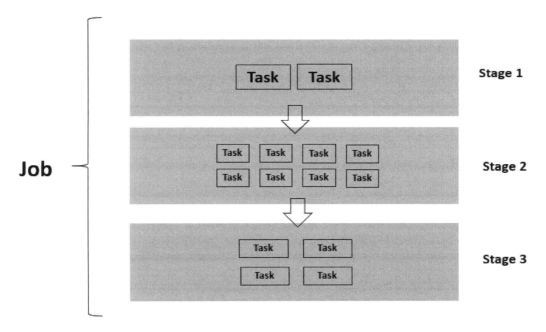

Figure 1.4 – Jobs, stages, and tasks

As a rule of thumb, the total number of partitions should always be in the multiples of the total slots in the cluster. For instance, if a cluster has 16 slots and the data has 16 partitions, then each slot receives 1 task that processes 1 partition. But instead, if there are 15 partitions, then 1 slot will remain empty. This leads to the state of cluster underutilization. In the case of 17 partitions, a job will take twice the time to complete as it will wait for that 1 extra task to finish processing.

Let's move on from Spark for now and get acquainted with Databricks.

Introducing Databricks

Databricks provides a collaborative platform for data engineering and data science. Powered by the potential of Apache Spark™, Databricks helps enable ML at scale. It has also revolutionized the existing data lakes by introducing the **Lakehouse** architecture. You can refer to the following published whitepaper to learn about the Lakehouse architecture in detail: `http://cidrdb.org/cidr2021/papers/cidr2021_paper17.pdf`.

Irrespective of the data role in any industry, Databricks has something for everybody:

- **Data engineer**: Create **ETL** and **ELT** pipelines to run big data workloads.
- **Data scientist**: Perform exploratory data analysis and train ML models at scale.
- **Data analyst**: Perform big data analytics harnessing the power of Apache Spark.
- **Business intelligence analyst**: Build powerful dashboards using Databricks SQL Analytics.

Databricks and Spark together provide a unified platform for big data processing in the cloud. This is possible because Spark is a compute engine that remains decoupled from storage. Spark in Databricks combines ETL, ML, and real-time streaming with collaborative notebooks. Processing in Databricks can scale to petabytes of data and thousands of nodes in no time!

Spark can connect to any number of data sources, including Amazon S3, Azure Data Lake, **HDFS**, Kafka, and many more. As Databricks lives in the cloud, spinning up a Spark cluster is possible with the click of a button. We do not need to worry about setting up infrastructure to use Databricks. This enables us to focus on the data at hand and continue solving problems.

Currently, Databricks is available on all four major cloud platforms, **Amazon Web Services** (**AWS**), **Microsoft Azure**, **Google Cloud Platform**, and **Alibaba Cloud**. In this book, we will be working on **Azure Databricks** with the **standard pricing tier**. Databricks is a first-party service in Azure and is deeply integrated with the complete Azure ecosystem.

Since Azure Databricks is a cloud-native managed service, there is a cost associated with its usage. To view the Databricks pricing, check out `https://azure.microsoft.com/en-in/pricing/details/databricks/`.

Creating an Azure Databricks workspace

To create a Databricks instance in Azure, we will need an **Azure subscription** and a **resource group**. An Azure subscription is a gateway to Microsoft's cloud services. It entitles us to create and use Azure's services. A resource group in Azure is equivalent to a logical container that hosts the different services. To create an Azure Databricks instance, we need to complete the following steps:

1. Go to Azure's website, `portal.azure.com`, and log in with your credentials.

2. In the **Navigate** section, click on **Resource groups** and then **Create**.

3. In **Subscription**, set the name of the Azure subscription, set a suitable name in **Resource group**, set **Region**, and click on **Review + create**.

4. A **Validation passed** message will flash at the top; then, click on **Create**. Once the resource group is created, a notification will pop up saying **Resource group created**. Following the message, click on **Go to resource group**.

5. This opens an empty resource group. Now it is time to create a Databricks instance. Click on **Create** and select **Marketplace**. In the search bar, type `Azure Databricks` and select it from the drop-down menu. Click on **Create**.

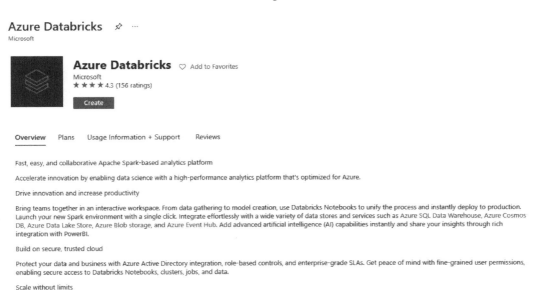

Figure 1.5 – Creating Azure Databricks

6.   Set **Subscription**, **Resource group**, a name, **Region**, and **Pricing Tier** (**Standard**, **Premium**, or **Trial**). In this book, we will be working with the standard pricing tier of Azure Databricks.

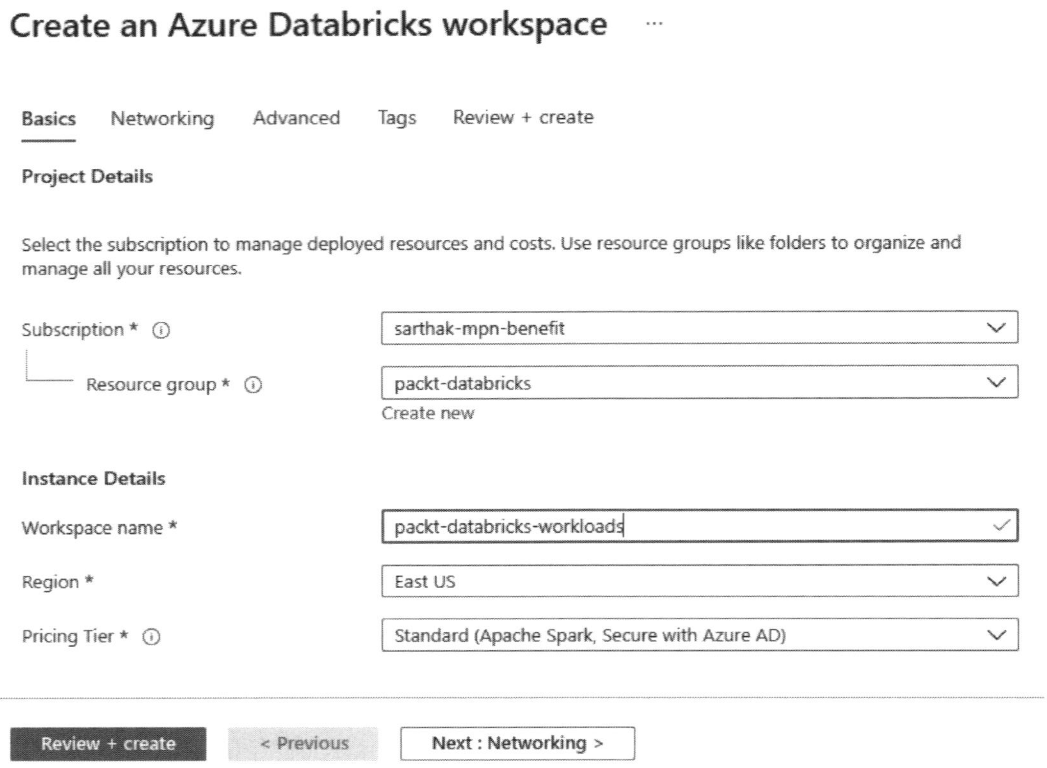

Create an Azure Databricks workspace   ···

Basics   Networking   Advanced   Tags   Review + create

Project Details

Select the subscription to manage deployed resources and costs. Use resource groups like folders to organize and manage all your resources.

Subscription * ⓘ	sarthak-mpn-benefit ⌄
Resource group * ⓘ	packt-databricks ⌄
	Create new

Instance Details

Workspace name *	packt-databricks-workloads ✓
Region *	East US ⌄
Pricing Tier * ⓘ	Standard (Apache Spark, Secure with Azure AD) ⌄

[Review + create]   [< Previous]   [Next : Networking >]

Figure 1.6 – Creating an Azure Databricks workspace

7.   Click on **Next : Networking**. We will not be creating Databricks in a **VNet**. So, keep both the options toggled to **No**. Finally, click on **Review + create**. Once the validation is successful, click on **Create**. It takes a few minutes for the Databricks instance to get created. Once the deployment is complete, click on **Go to Resource**. To launch the Databricks workspace, click on **Launch Workspace**.

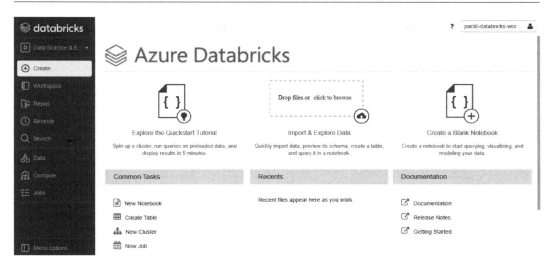

Figure 1.7 – Azure Databricks workspace

Now that we have a workspace up and running, let's explore how we can apply it to different concepts.

Core Databricks concepts

The Databricks workspace menu is displayed on the left pane. We can configure the menu based on our workloads, **Data Science and Engineering** or **Machine Learning**. Let's start with the former. We will learn more about the ML functionalities in *Chapter 3, Learning about Machine Learning and Graph Processing with Databricks*. The menu consists of the following:

- **Workspace**: A repository with a folder-like structure that contains all the Azure Databricks assets. These assets include the following:

  - **Notebooks**: An interface that holds code, visualizations, and markdown text. Notebooks can also be imported and exported from the Databricks workspace.

  - **Library**: A package of commands made available to a notebook or a Databricks job.

  - **Dashboard**: A structured representation of the selective visualizations used in a notebook.

  - **Folder**: A logical grouping of related assets in the workspace.

- **Repos**: This provides integration with Git providers such as GitHub, Bitbucket, GitLab, and Azure DevOps.

- **Recents**: Displays the most recently used notebooks in the Databricks workspace.

- **Search**: The search bar helps us to find assets in the workspace.

- **Data**: This is the data management tab that is built on top of a Hive metastore. Here, we can find all the Hive tables registered in the workspace. The Hive metastore stores all the metadata information, such as column details, storage path, and partitions, but not the actual data that resides in a cloud storage location. The tables are queried using Apache Spark APIs including Python, Scala, R, and SQL. Like any data warehouse, we need to create a database and then register the Hive tables.

- **Compute**: This is where we interact with the Spark cluster. It is further divided into three categories:

    - **All-Purpose Clusters**: These are used to run Databricks notebooks and jobs. An all-purpose cluster can also be shared among users in the workspace. You can manually terminate or restart an all-purpose cluster.

    - **Job Clusters**: These are created by the Azure Databricks job scheduler when a new job is created. Once the job is complete, it is automatically terminated. It is not possible to restart a job cluster.

    - **Pools**: A pool is a set of idle node instances that help reduce cluster start up and autoscaling times. When a cluster is attached to a pool, it acquires the driver and worker instances from within the pool.

Figure 1.8 – Clusters in Azure Databricks

- **Jobs**: A job is a mechanism that helps to schedule notebooks for creating data pipelines.

Now that we have an understanding of the core concepts of Databricks, let's create our first Spark cluster!

Creating a Spark cluster

It is time to create our first cluster! In the following steps, we will create an all-purpose cluster and later attach it to a notebook. We will be discussing cluster configurations in detail in *Chapter 4, Managing Spark Clusters*:

1. Select the **Clusters** tab and click on **Create Cluster**. Give an appropriate name to the cluster.

2. Set **Cluster Mode** to **Standard**. **Standard** cluster mode is ideal when there is a single user for the cluster. **High Concurrency** mode is recommended for concurrent users, but it does not support Scala. A **Single Node** cluster has no worker nodes and is only suitable for small data volumes.

3. Leave the **Pool** option as **None** and **Databricks Runtime Version** as the default value. The Databricks runtime version decides the Spark version and configurations for the cluster.

4. For **Autopilot Options**, disable the **Enable autoscaling** checkbox. Autoscaling helps the cluster to automatically scale between the maximum and minimum number of worker nodes. In the second autopilot option, replace **120** with **030** to terminate the cluster after 30 minutes of inactivity.

5. We can leave the **Worker Type** and **Driver Type** options as their default values. Set the number of workers to 01. Keep the **Spot instances** checkbox disabled. When enabled, the cluster uses Azure Spot VMs to save costs.

6.   Click on **Create Cluster**.

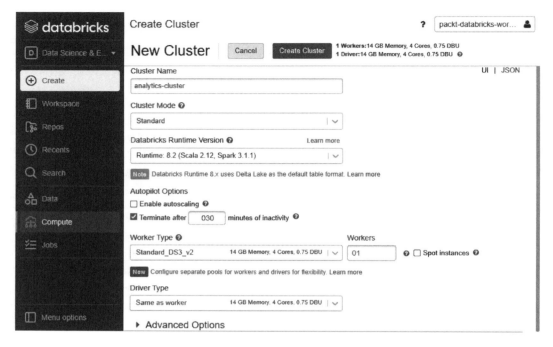

Figure 1.9 – Initializing a Databricks cluster

With the Spark cluster initialized, let's create our first Databricks notebook!

Databricks notebooks

Now we'll create our first Databricks notebook. On the left pane menu, click on **Create** and select **Notebook**. Give a suitable name to the notebook, keep the **Default Language** option as **Python**, set **Cluster**, and click on **Create**.

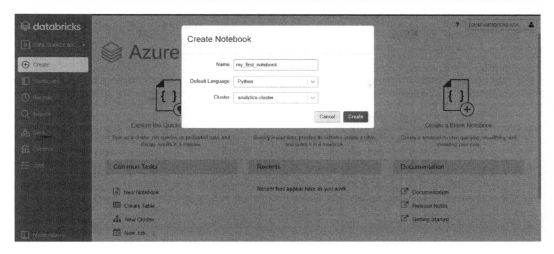

Figure 1.10 – Creating a Databricks notebook

We can create documentation cells to independently run blocks of code. A new cell can be created with the click of a button. For people who have worked with **Jupyter Notebooks**, this interface might look familiar.

We can also execute code in different languages right inside one notebook. For example, the first notebook that we've created has a default language of Python, but we can also run code in Scala, SQL, and R in the same notebook! This is made possible with the help of magic commands. We need to specify the magic command at the beginning of a new cell:

- **Python**: `%python` or `%py`
- **R**: `%r`
- **Scala**: `%scala`
- **SQL**: `%sql`

> **Note**
>
> The `%pip` magic command can also be used in Databricks notebooks to manage notebook-scoped libraries.

Let us look at executing code in multiple languages in the following image:

Figure 1.11 – Executing code in multiple languages

We can also render a cell as **Markdown** using the %md magic command. This allows us to add rendered text between cells of code.

Databricks notebooks also support rendering HTML graphics using the displayHTML function. Currently, this feature is only supported for Python, R, and Scala notebooks. To use the function, we need to pass in HTML, CSS, or JavaScript code:

Figure 1.12 – Rendering HTML in a notebook

We can use the %sh magic command to run shell commands on the driver node.

Databricks provides a **Databricks Utilities (dbutils)** module to perform tasks collectively. With dbutils, we can work with external storage, parametrize notebooks, and handle secrets. To list the available functionalities of dbutils, we can run dbutils.help() in a Python or Scala notebook.

The notebooks consist of another feature called **widgets**. These widgets help to add parameters to a notebook and are made available with the dbutils module. By default, widgets are visible at the top of a notebook and are categorized as follows:

- **Text**: Input the string value in a textbox.
- **Dropdown**: Select a value from a list.
- **Combobox**: Combination of text and drop-down widgets.

- **Multiselect**: Select one or more values from a list:

Figure 1.13 – Notebook widget example. Here, we create a text widget,
fetch its value, and call it in a print statement

We can also run one notebook inside another using the `%run` magic command. The magic command must be followed by the notebook path.

Figure 1.14 – Using the %run magic command

Databricks File System (DBFS)

DBFS is a filesystem mounted in every Databricks workspace for temporary storage. It is an abstraction on top of a scalable object store in the cloud. For instance, in the case of Azure Databricks, the DBFS is built on top of **Azure Blob Storage**. But this is managed for us, so we needn't worry too much about how and where the DBFS is actually located. All we need to understand is how can we use DBFS inside a Databricks workspace.

DBFS helps us in the following ways:

- We can persist data to DBFS so that it is not lost after the termination of the cluster.
- DBFS allows us to mount object storage such as Azure Data Lake or Azure Blob Storage in the workspace. This makes it easy to access data without requiring credentials every time.
- We can access and interact with the data using the directory semantics instead of using URLs for object storage.

DBFS has a default storage location called the **DBFS root**. We can access DBFS in several ways:

- With the `%fs` magic command: We can use the `%fs` command in a notebook cell.

- With `dbutils`: We can call the `dbutils` module to access the DBFS. Using `dbutils.fs.ls("<path>")` is equivalent to running `%fs ls <path>`. Here, `<path>` is a DBFS path. Both these commands list the directories in a specific DBFS "path."

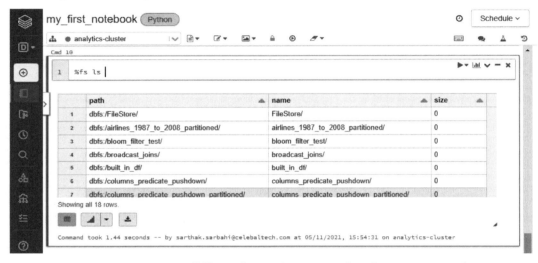

Figure 1.15 – Listing all files in the DBFS root using the %fs magic command

> **Note**
>
> We need to enclose `dbutils.fs.ls("path")` in Databricks' `display()` function to obtain a rendered output.

Databricks jobs

A Databricks job helps to run and automate activities such as an ETL job or a data analytics task. A job can be executed either immediately or on a scheduled basis. A job can be created by using the UI or CLI or invoking the Jobs UI. We will now create a job using the Databricks UI:

1. Create a new Databricks Python notebook with the name `jobs-notebook` and paste the following code in a new cell. This code creates a new delta table and inserts records into the table. We'll learn about Delta Lake in more detail later in this chapter. Note that the following two code blocks must be run in the same cell.

The following code block creates a delta table in Databricks with the name of insurance_claims. The table has four columns, user_id, city, country, and amount:

```sql
%sql
-- Creating a delta table and storing data in DBFS
-- Our table's name is 'insurance_claims' and has four
columns
CREATE OR REPLACE TABLE insurance_claims (
  user_id INT NOT NULL,
  city STRING NOT NULL,
  country STRING NOT NULL,
  amount INT NOT NULL
)
USING DELTA
LOCATION 'dbfs:/tmp/insurance_claims';
```

Now, we will insert five records into the table. In the following code block, every INSERT INTO statement inserts one new record into the delta table:

```sql
INSERT INTO insurance_claims (user_id, city, country,
amount)
VALUES (100, 'Mumbai', 'India', 200000);
INSERT INTO insurance_claims (user_id, city, country,
amount)
VALUES (101, 'Delhi', 'India', 400000);
INSERT INTO insurance_claims (user_id, city, country,
amount)
VALUES (102, 'Chennai', 'India', 100000);
INSERT INTO insurance_claims (user_id, city, country,
amount)
VALUES (103, 'Bengaluru', 'India', 700000);
```

2. On the workspace menu, click on **Jobs** and then **Create Job**. Give a name to the job and keep **Schedule Type** as **Manual (Paused)**. Under the **Task** heading, set **Type** to **Notebook**, select the jobs-notebook notebook that we created, and in **Cluster**, select an existing all-purpose cluster.

3. Keep **Maximum Concurrent Runs** at the default value of **1**. Under **Alerts**, click on **Add**. Add the email address to which alerts must be sent and select **Success** and **Failure**. This will ensure that the designated email address will be notified upon a job success or failure.

4. Click on **Create**. Once the job is created, click on **Runs** and select **Run Now**.

5. As soon as the job completes, we will receive an email informing us whether the job succeeded or failed. If the job is in progress, we can find more information about the current run under **Active Runs**.

6. When the job finishes, a new record will be added under **Completed Runs (past 60 days)** giving the start time, mode of launch, duration of run, and status of run.

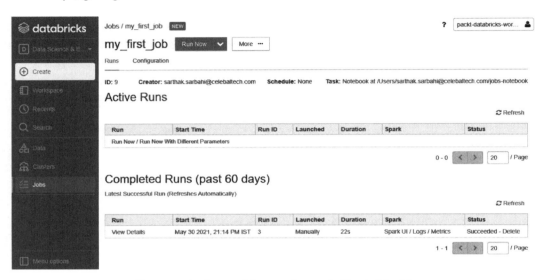

Figure 1.16 – Successful manual run of a Databricks job

Databricks Community

Databricks Community is a platform that provides a free-of-cost Databricks workspace. It supports a single node cluster wherein we have one driver and no workers. The community platform is great for beginners to get started with Databricks. But several features of Azure Databricks are not supported in the Community edition. For example, we cannot create jobs or change cluster configuration settings. To sign up for Databricks Community, visit https://community.cloud.databricks.com/login.html.

Learning about Delta Lake

Delta Lake was launched by Databricks as an open source project owned by the Linux Foundation that converts a traditional data lake into a lakehouse. The term *lakehouse* refers to a platform that brings in the best of both data lakes and warehouses. Delta Lake offers the following features:

- **ACID transactions**: Data readers never see inconsistent data, also called *dirty reads*.

- **Handling metadata**: Spark's distributed processing power makes it easy to handle the metadata of tables with terabytes and petabytes of data in a scalable fashion.

- **Streaming and batch workloads**: Delta Lake helps unify stream and batch processing on data.

- **Schema enforcement**: The schema is always checked before data gets appended. This helps to prevent the corruption of data.

- **Time travel**: View and roll back to previous versions of data enabling audit logs.

- **Upserts and deletes**: Perform transactions such as updates, inserts, and deletes on data lying in the lake.

Next, we'll look at big data file formats.

Big data file formats

Before we dive deeper into Delta Lake, let's first try to understand the file formats used to store big data. Traditional file formats such as CSV and TSV store data in a row-wise format and are not partitioned. CSVs are basically strings without any data types so they always need to be scanned entirely without any scope for filtering. This makes it difficult for processing and querying larger datasets. Instead, file formats such as **Parquet**, **ORC**, and **Avro** help us overcome many such challenges as they can be stored in a distributed fashion.

> **Note**
>
> Row-based file formats store data by row, whereas columnar file formats store data by column. Row-based file formats work best for transactional writes of data, whereas columnar file formats are ideal for data querying and analytical workloads.

Let us look at row-based file formats versus columnar file formats in the following image:

Row-Based (CSV, TSV, and AVRO)

	User ID	Name	City	Age
Row 1	100	Peter	Paris	39
Row 2	101	Thomas	New York	21
Row 3	102	Drew	Singapore	44
Row 4	103	Varun	Mumbai	27

Columnar (Parquet, Delta, and ORC)

	Row 1	Row 2	Row 3	Row 4
User ID	100	101	102	103
Name	Peter	Thomas	Drew	Varun
City	Paris	New York	Singapore	Mumbai
Age	39	21	44	27

Figure 1.17 – Row-based file formats versus columnar

The similarities between Parquet, ORC, and Avro are as follows:

- All three file formats are machine-readable formats and not human-readable.
- They can be partitioned across a cluster for parallel processing and distribution.
- The formats carry the data schema as well. This helps newer machines or clusters to process the data independently.

The differences between Parquet, ORC, and Avro are as follows:

Parameter	Avro	Parquet	ORC
Read or Write	Best Suited for Writing Data	Best Suited for Reading Data	Best Suited for Reading Data
Row-Based or Columnar	Row-Based	Columnar	Columnar
Most Compatible Platforms	Kafka and Druid	Spark, Arrow, and Impala	Hive and Presto
Compression	Low	High	High

Figure 1.18 – Comparison of Avro, Parquet, and ORC

Coming back to Delta Lake, it can simply be treated as a file format. Tables that are created on top of this delta file format are simply called **delta tables**. The delta file format is mainly composed of two components:

- **Transactional logs**: A `_delta_log` folder is created when data is written in the delta file format. This folder stores files that record all the transactions to data.

- **Versioned Parquet files**: This is the actual data that is written out as partitions. These Parquet partition files (`.parquet`) can also be compacted later using different functions. For efficient querying purposes, these Parquet partition files can also be distributed based on partition folders.

Name	Modified	Access tier	Blob type	Size
[..]				
_delta_log				
_delta_log	4/28/2021, 11:50:42 AM	Hot (Inferred)	Block blob	0 B
part-00000-5d15c033-1a01-4998-bdc6-6433a03586e8-c000.snappy.parquet	4/28/2021, 11:47:02 AM	Hot (Inferred)	Block blob	34.5 MiB
part-00000-7c824cbe-3c20-4e6f-a6e0-8de1f1586e61-c000.snappy.parquet	4/28/2021, 11:42:16 AM	Hot (Inferred)	Block blob	563.58 MiB
part-00000-dfc038c8-ff7f-4d23-b7ec-7a254d68868f-c000.snappy.parquet	4/28/2021, 11:50:40 AM	Hot (Inferred)	Block blob	563.58 MiB
part-00000-eace6194-d193-4ae3-a1ba-f5b5468a43d4-c000.snappy.parquet	4/28/2021, 11:31:15 AM	Hot (Inferred)	Block blob	34.5 MiB
part-00001-5d142d03-17a8-4d74-b8c4-45ef8f6d807a-c000.snappy.parquet	4/28/2021, 11:47:02 AM	Hot (Inferred)	Block blob	34.39 MiB
part-00001-9fcd23bf-4f82-4990-96e4-c2bdfd3d1ee9-c000.snappy.parquet	4/28/2021, 11:31:15 AM	Hot (Inferred)	Block blob	34.39 MiB
part-00002-535070f3-36d9-49d6-813f-f53f7664c3bf-c000.snappy.parquet	4/28/2021, 11:31:15 AM	Hot (Inferred)	Block blob	34.04 MiB
part-00002-e8bb7785-9477-4494-9699-b3ca89082ece-c000.snappy.parquet	4/28/2021, 11:47:02 AM	Hot (Inferred)	Block blob	34.04 MiB

Figure 1.19 – Data written in delta format as viewed in Azure Blob Storage

It's also important for us to understand the use and value of the transactional log.

Understanding the transactional log

Having an understanding of the transactional log is imperative when working with Delta Lake. Let's take a peek at the contents of the _delta_log folder.

Name	Modified	Access tier	Blob type	Size	Lease state
[..]					
_tmp_path_dir	4/28/2021, 11:50:42 ...	Hot (Inferred)	Block blob	0 B	Available
00000000000000000000.crc	4/28/2021, 11:31:57 ...	Hot (Inferred)	Block blob	95 B	Available
00000000000000000000.json	4/28/2021, 11:31:55 ...	Hot (Inferred)	Block blob	48.53 KiB	Available
00000000000000000001.crc	4/28/2021, 11:42:18 ...	Hot (Inferred)	Block blob	94 B	Available
00000000000000000001.json	4/28/2021, 11:42:16 ...	Hot (Inferred)	Block blob	6.73 KiB	Available
00000000000000000002.crc	4/28/2021, 11:47:43 ...	Hot (Inferred)	Block blob	95 B	Available
00000000000000000002.json	4/28/2021, 11:47:41 ...	Hot (Inferred)	Block blob	45.76 KiB	Available
00000000000000000003.crc	4/28/2021, 11:50:42 ...	Hot (Inferred)	Block blob	94 B	Available
00000000000000000003.json	4/28/2021, 11:50:41 ...	Hot (Inferred)	Block blob	6.84 KiB	Available

Figure 1.20 – Contents of the _delta_log folder as viewed in Azure Blob Storage

Whenever a transaction is carried out on a delta table, the changes are recorded in the _delta_log folder in the form of JSON files. The naming conventions of these JSON files begin sequentially, starting with 000000.json. Subsequent JSON files are created as changes get committed (000001.json, 000002.json, and so on). Also, with each fresh transaction, a new set of Parquet files may be written. In this process, the new JSON file created in the _delta_log folder keeps a record of which Parquet files to reference and which to omit. This happens because every transaction to a delta table results in a new version of the table.

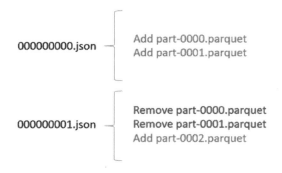

Figure 1.21 – JSON files in _delta_log

Let's see how this works with an example. Suppose we have a delta table with a `_delta_log` folder containing `00000.json`. Suppose this JSON file references two Parquet files, `part-0000.parquet` and `part-0001.parquet`.

Now we have an UPDATE transaction carried out on the delta table. This creates a new JSON file in the `_delta_log` folder by the name of `00001.json`. Also, a new Parquet file is added in the delta table's directory, `part-0002.parquet`. Upon checking the new JSON file, we find that it references `part-0001.parquet` and `part-0002.parquet` but omits `part-0000.parquet`.

Delta Lake in action

Let's start by creating a Spark DataFrame by reading a CSV file. Create a new Databricks Python notebook and spin up a Spark cluster with one driver, one worker, the standard type, and autoscaling disabled. Every code block in the following section must be executed in a new notebook cell:

1. We will be using the `airlines` dataset from the `databricks-datasets` repository. Databricks provides many sample datasets in every workspace. These are part of the `databricks-datasets` directory of the DBFS. The following code block creates a new Spark DataFrame by specifying the first row as the header, automatically inferring the schema, and reading from a CSV file. Once the DataFrame is created, we will display the first five rows:

```
airlines = (spark.read
            .option("header",True)
            .option("inferSchema",True)
            .option("delimiter",",")
            .csv("dbfs:/databricks-datasets/airlines/
part-00000")
# View the dataframe
display(airlines.limit(5))
```

2. Next, we will write the DataFrame as a delta file in the DBFS. Once the writing process is complete, we can look at the contents of the delta file. It contains four Parquet files and a `_delta_log` folder:

```
airlines.write.mode("overwrite").format("delta").
save("dbfs:/airlines/")
```

We can view the location where the data is written in delta format:

```
display(dbutils.fs.ls("dbfs:/airlines/"))
```

3. Inside the `_delta_log` folder, we can find one JSON file:

```
display(dbutils.fs.ls("dbfs:/airlines/_delta_log/"))
```

4. Now, we will create a delta table using the delta file that is written to Azure Blob Storage. Here, we will switch from PySpark to Spark SQL syntax using the `%sql` magic command. The name of the delta table created is `airlines_delta_table`. A count operation on the newly created delta table returns the number of records in the table:

```
%sql
DROP TABLE IF EXISTS airlines_delta_table;
CREATE TABLE airlines_delta_table USING DELTA LOCATION
"dbfs:/airlines/";
%sql
SELECT COUNT(*) as count FROM airlines_delta_table
```

5. Let's perform a DELETE operation on the delta table. This will delete all the rows where the `Month` column equals `10`. This deletes 448,620 rows from the delta table:

```
%sql
DELETE FROM airlines_delta_table WHERE Month = '10'
```

6. Next, we will perform an UPDATE operation on the delta table. This transaction will update the `Dest` column and replace all the `SFO` values with `San Francisco`. We can also see that 7,575 rows received updates in the table:

```
%sql
UPDATE airlines_delta_table SET Dest = 'San Francisco'
WHERE Dest = 'SFO'
```

7. Before we move forward, let's look at the Parquet files and transactional logs folder once again. Inside the delta file, we can see that more Parquet files have been added after two transactions (DELETE and UPDATE) were carried out:

```
display(dbutils.fs.ls("dbfs:/airlines/"))
```

8. Also, the `_delta_log` folder now contains two more JSON files, one for each transaction:

```
display(dbutils.fs.ls("dbfs:/airlines/_delta_log/"))
```

9. Finally, it is time for time travel! Running the DESCRIBE HISTORY command on the delta table returns a list of all the versions of the table:

```sql
%sql
-- Time travel
DESCRIBE HISTORY airlines_delta_table
```

10. Switching to a previous version is as easy as adding VERSION AS OF to the delta table. First, we'll try to query the data based on the condition that got updated. For instance, after the update operation, no record should have the SFO value. Hence, we get a count of 0:

```sql
%sql
-- Return count of rows where Dest = 'SFO' in current
version that is version 2
SELECT COUNT(*) FROM airlines_delta_table WHERE Dest =
'SFO'
```

11. But when the same query is run on the previous version of the delta table (version 1), we get a count of 7,575. This is because this SQL query is querying on the data that existed before the update operation:

```sql
%sql
-- Return count of rows where Dest = 'SFO' in version 1
SELECT COUNT(*) FROM airlines_delta_table VERSION AS OF 1
WHERE Dest = 'SFO'
```

Let's recap what we've covered in this first chapter.

Summary

In this chapter, we learned about the fundamentals of Spark, got an introduction to Databricks, and explored Delta Lake. We were introduced to Azure Databricks and the important workspace components. We learned how to create an Azure Databricks instance, a notebook in the Databricks workspace, Spark clusters, and Databricks jobs. We also learned about the important big data file formats such as Parquet, Avro, and ORC. We also learned about the fundamentals of Delta Lake and went through a worked-out example.

In the next chapter, we will dive deeper into the concepts of batch and stream processing in Azure Databricks. We'll also see more examples in the chapter to practice working hands-on in a Databricks environment.

2
Batch and Real-Time Processing in Databricks

Azure Databricks is capable of processing batch and real-time big data workloads using **Apache Spark™**. As data engineers, it is important to master these workloads for building real-world use cases. A batch load generally refers to an **ETL (Extract, Transform, Load)** or **ELT (Extract, Load, Transform)** process where large chunks of data get copied from a *source* to a *sink*. This type of workload can take time to process, ranging from minutes to hours, whereas real-time processing works with a much smaller latency (that is, seconds or even milliseconds).

When it comes to Databricks, there are different ways to process batch and real-time workloads. In this chapter, we will discuss the approaches to build and run these workloads. The topics covered in this chapter are as follows:

- Differentiating batch versus real-time processing
- Mounting **Azure Data Lake** in Databricks
- Working with batch processing
- Batch ETL process demo
- Learning Structured Streaming in Azure Databricks

Technical requirements

To follow the hands-on examples in the chapter, the following are required:

- An Azure subscription with a Databricks resource deployed and permission to create **Azure** storage accounts
- Access to **Azure Active Directory** (**Azure AD**) and permission to create service principal applications
- Databricks notebooks and a Spark cluster
- Privileges to add role assignments in Azure resources

Code samples from `https://github.com/PacktPublishing/Optimiz-ing-Databricks-Workload/tree/main/Chapter02`

Differentiating batch versus real-time processing

Batch processing means processing chunks of data in a fixed interval of time. A *batch process*, also called a *batch load*, takes a considerable amount of time and compute. For example, an ETL script reading 500 GB of data from a source, transforming it, and writing to a sink at a 12-hour frequency, works as a batch process.

But a *real-time process* performs computation on a continuous stream of data. In other words, a real-time stream processes data as soon as it arrives. In the case of Spark, its **Structured Streaming** API is used to process data in real-time.

The following table illustrates the differences between batch and real-time processing in Databricks.

Parameter	Batch processing	Real-time processing
Spark cluster	Active only during process execution	Remains active throughout
Spark job runtime	Not very critical (minutes to hours)	Very critical (milliseconds to seconds)
Sorting data	Performed after job completion	Not required
Spark API involved	Spark DataFrames API	Spark Structured Streaming
Source and Sink	Databases, data lakes, data warehouses, and so on	Data ingestion frameworks/services, data lakes, and object storage

Figure 2.1 – Batch and real-time processing comparison in Databricks

We will start our learning journey with batch processing and then proceed to real-time streaming.

Mounting Azure Data Lake in Databricks

Azure Data Lake (storage account) is a limitless data lake service managed by **Microsoft**. It allows the storage and analysis of big data of all forms: *structured*, *semi-structured*, and *unstructured*. It is built to accommodate big data analytics by integrating with **Hadoop** and Spark. We will be using Azure Data Lake quite often in this book. So, it is important for us to learn its integration with Azure Databricks.

Creating an Azure Data Lake instance

Now, we will create an Azure Data Lake instance and use it as our primary data store in the Azure environment:

1. Go to Azure's website (`portal.azure.com`) and sign in to the portal. Open an existing **resource group**, then click on **Create** and then on **Marketplace**. Search for `Storage account`. The following window opens up:

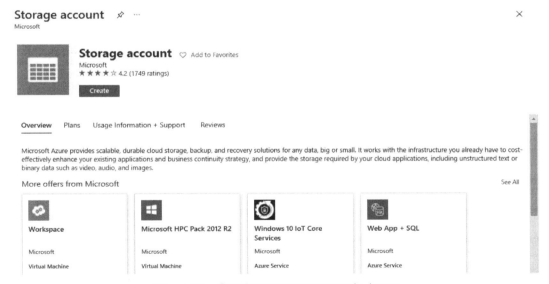

Figure 2.2 – Creating a storage account in Azure

2. Click on **Create**. Set the **Resource group**, **Storage account name**, and **Region**. Set **Performance** to **Standard: Recommended for most scenarios (general-purpose v2 account)**. Set **Redundancy** to **Locally-redundant storage (LRS)** from the drop-down options. Click on **Next: Advanced >**.

3. Click on the checkbox next to **Enable hierarchical namespace**. We can keep the rest of the settings as their default values. Click on **Review + create**. Click on **Create**.

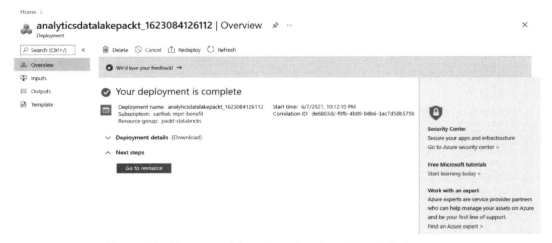

Figure 2.3 – The successful creation of an Azure Data Lake instance

This completes the creation of our Azure Data Lake instance. Next, we'll talk about accessing **ADLS (Azure Data Lake Storage)** in Databricks.

Accessing Azure Data Lake in Databricks

We will be securely accessing data from the data lake in Databricks. This is made possible by using **OAuth 2.0** with an Azure AD service principal application. This provides us with a mount point to files and folders in the data lake. Let's start by creating an Azure AD service principal application:

1. Go to the data lake created in the previous step. Click on **Containers**. Click on **+ Container** to create a new one. Give it a suitable name and set the **Public access level** to **Private (no anonymous access)**. Click on **Create**.

2. In the search bar at the top, search for `Azure Active Directory`. Click on **App registrations** on the left pane. Click on **+ New registration**. Give a name to the application and click on **Register**. Note down the details from the **Application (client) ID** and **Directory (tenant) ID** sections for later use. This completes the process of creating a service principal application.

3. On the same page, click on **Certificates and Secrets**. Click on **+ New client secret** and enter a suitable description in the **Description** field. Leave the **Expires** option at its default value. Click on **Add**. Note down the details in the **Value** section of the newly created secret for later use.

4. Go back to the storage account and click on **Access Control (IAM)**. Click on **+ Add** and select **Add role assignment**. If this option is disabled, you need to contact the Azure subscription's administrator. In **Role**, set **Storage Blob Data Contributor**, in **Assign access to**, set **User, group, or service principal**, and under **Select**, type the name of the service principal application and click on it. Click on **Save**.

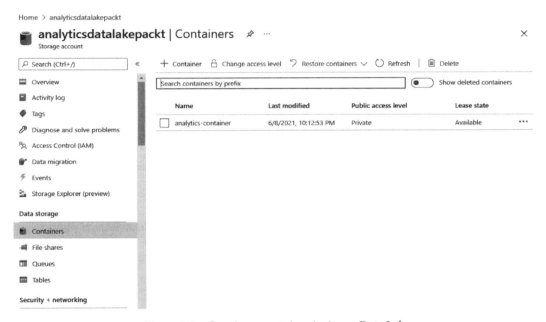

Figure 2.4 – Creating a container in Azure Data Lake

5. Open a Databricks workspace, start a cluster, and create a new notebook. Now, we will run some **PySpark** code to finish mounting the data lake on Databricks.

6. In a new cell of the notebook, enter the following code block:

```
configs = {"fs.azure.account.auth.type": "OAuth",
        "fs.azure.account.oauth.provider.
type": "org.apache.hadoop.fs.azurebfs.oauth2.
ClientCredsTokenProvider",
        "fs.azure.account.oauth2.client.id":
"<application-id>",
```

```
            "fs.azure.account.oauth2.client.secret":
"<application-client-secret-value>",
            "fs.azure.account.oauth2.client.endpoint":
"https://login.microsoftonline.com/<directory-id>/oauth2/
token"}
dbutils.fs.mount(
    source = "abfss://<container-name>@<storage-account-
name>.dfs.core.windows.net/",
    mount_point = "/mnt/<mount-name>",
    extra_configs = configs)
```

In the preceding code block, the following replacements need to be made:

I.   <application-id>: Service principal application (client) ID

II.   <application-client-secret-value>: Service principal application client secret value

III. <directory-id>: Directory (tenant) ID

IV.   <container-name>: Name of the container of Azure Data Lake

V.   <storage-account-name>: Name of the Azure Data Lake

VI.   <mount-point>: Mount point name

7. After making these replacements, run the notebook cell. After running for a few seconds, the cell will return True. This confirms that the data lake has been successfully mounted on the Databricks workspace. To further clarify this, run the %fs mounts command in a new cell and look for the mount point name in the **mountPoint** column:

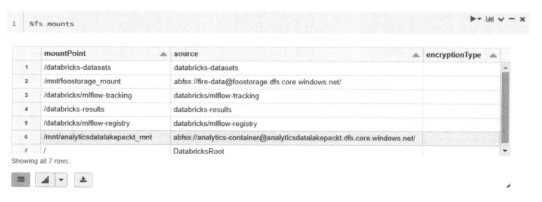

Figure 2.5 – Viewing all the mount points in the Databricks workspace

> **Note**
>
> Instead of exposing credentials in code, it is better to store them in **Azure Key Vault**. Azure Key Vault integrates with the Databricks Secrets API to retrieve secrets and credentials in a secure fashion. The Secrets API allows us to manage secrets and secret scopes, and it also allows us to access permissions. For reference, please check out the following link: `https://docs.microsoft.com/en-us/azure/databricks/dev-tools/api/latest/secrets`.

Working with batch processing

We will now begin learning the essential PySpark code to read, transform, and write data. Any ETL script begins with reading from a source, transforming the data, and then writing data to a sink. Let's begin with reading data from **DBFS (Databricks File System)** for a batch process.

Reading data

Run the following command in a new cell in a notebook:

```
%fs ls dbfs:/databricks-datasets/
```

This will display a list of sample datasets mounted by the Databricks team for learning and testing purposes. The dataset that we will be working with resides in the DBFS path, `dbfs:/databricks-datasets/asa/airlines/`. This dataset describes different airlines' **on-time performance** and consists of about 120 million records!

1. Run the `%fs ls dbfs:/databricks-datasets/asa/airlines/` command, and we can see that the path contains 22 CSV files. Their corresponding sizes are also mentioned in *bytes*. We will now read all the CSV files at once by specifying a * after the path.

2. Paste the following syntax in a new cell and run the cell. Note the * after the path.

    Read the CSV files to create a Spark DataFrame:

    ```
    airlines_1987_to_2008 = (
    spark
    .read
    .option("header",True)
    .option("delimiter",",")
    .option("inferSchema",True)
    .csv("dbfs:/databricks-datasets/asa/airlines/*")
    )
    ```

View the DataFrame:

```
display(airlines_1987_to_2008)
```

The preceding code reads all the CSV files in the DBFS path, creates a Spark DataFrame named `airlines_1987_to_2008`, and then displays the first 1,000 rows of the DataFrame:

```
1  # Read csv files to create Spark dataframe
2  airlines_1987_to_2008 = (spark.read.option("header",True).option("delimiter",",").option("inferSchema",True).csv("dbfs:/databricks-
   datasets/asa/airlines/*"))
3  # View the dataframe
4  display(airlines_1987_to_2008)
```

▸ (3) Spark Jobs

▸ ▣ airlines_1987_to_2008: pyspark.sql.dataframe.DataFrame = [Year: integer, Month: integer ... 27 more fields]

	Year ▲	Month ▲	DayofMonth ▲	DayOfWeek ▲	DepTime ▲	CRSDepTime ▲	ArrTime ▲	CRSArrTime ▲	UniqueCarrier ▲	FlightN
1	1988	1	9	6	1348	1331	1458	1435	PI	942
2	1988	1	10	7	1334	1331	1443	1435	PI	942
3	1988	1	11	1	1446	1331	1553	1435	PI	942
4	1988	1	12	2	1334	1331	1438	1435	PI	942
5	1988	1	13	3	1341	1331	1503	1435	PI	942
6	1988	1	14	4	1332	1331	1447	1435	PI	942
7	1988	1	15	5	1331	1331	1434	1435	PI	942

Showing the first 1000 rows.

Figure 2.6 – Reading and displaying the data in CSV files

The different variations of `option` in the preceding code are explained here:

I. `option("header",True)`: This specifies the first row of every CSV file as the common header of the DataFrame.

II. `option("delimiter",True)`: This instructs Spark to read all the files as comma-separated files.

III. `option("inferSchema",True)`: This scans all the CSV files to determine the most suitable data types for all the columns.

Now that we have read the data, let's check the number of records in the DataFrame.

Checking row count

Let's check the row count in the DataFrame. The syntax is `<dataframe>.count()`. Run the `airlines_1987_to_2008.count()` command in a new cell to check the number of rows:

```
1   # Return count of records in dataframe
2   airlines_1987_to_2008.count()
```

▸ (2) Spark Jobs

Out[3]: 123534969

Figure 2.7 – The DataFrame has more than 123 million rows!

Once we've read the data in a Spark DataFrame, we can apply a bunch of transformations. Let's look at them one by one.

Selecting columns

To select a few columns from the DataFrame, we can use the `select` DataFrame method. The syntax is `<dataframe>.select(<column_name>)`. Here, the following command returns the `Origin`, `Dest`, and `Distance` columns from the DataFrame:

```
display(airlines_1987_to_2008.
select("Origin","Dest","Distance"))
```

We need to enclose this in a `display()` function to get a rendered output in the notebook:

```
1   # Select the columns - Origin, Dest and Distance
2   display(airlines_1987_to_2008.select("Origin","Dest","Distance"))
```

▸ (1) Spark Jobs

	Origin	Dest	Distance
1	SMF	ONT	389
2	SMF	PDX	479
3	SMF	PDX	479
4	SMF	PDX	479
5	SMF	PDX	479
6	SMF	PDX	479
7	SMF	PHX	647

Showing the first 1000 rows.

Figure 2.8 – Selecting columns from a DataFrame

We have learned to select different columns from the DataFrame. Now, let's try filtering rows from the DataFrame.

Filtering data

To filter data from a DataFrame based on rows, we can use either the `where()` or `filter()` methods. The syntax is as follows:

- `where()`: `<dataframe>.where(<condition>)`
- `filter()`: `<dataframe>.filter(<condition>)`

To select a column inside these methods, we need a `col` function. This function helps us in defining the condition on that column. To use a `col` function, it is necessary to import the `pyspark.sql.functions` class. To import this class, we can run the `from pyspark.sql.functions import *` command. We can also chain several methods together. Let's try filtering for rows where the `Year` column equals `2001`. Do not forget to use the `display()` function:

- Import the class to use functions using the following code:

```
from pyspark.sql.functions import *
```

- Filter the data with the `where` method:

```
display(airlines_1987_to_2008.where(col("Year") == "2001"))
```

In Databricks, the preceding code appears as follows:

```
1   # Import the class to use functions
2   from pyspark.sql.functions import *
3   # Filtering data with 'where' method
4   display(airlines_1987_to_2008.where(col("Year") == "2001"))
```

▶ (4) Spark Jobs

	Year ▲	Month ▲	DayofMonth ▲	DayOfWeek ▲	DepTime ▲
1	2001	1	17	3	1806
2	2001	1	18	4	1805
3	2001	1	19	5	1821
4	2001	1	20	6	1807
5	2001	1	21	7	1810
6	2001	1	22	1	1807
7	2001	1	23	2	1802

Figure 2.9 – Filtering with the where method

Now, let's look at an example where we will chain the `select()` and `filter()` methods. We will select a few columns and then filter the data from that result:

- Chain the example using the `filter` method:

```
display(airlines_1987_to_2008.
select("Year","Origin","Dest").filter(col("Year") ==
"2001"))
```

In Databricks, the preceding code appears as follows:

```
1   # Chaining example and using 'filter' method
2   display(airlines_1987_to_2008.select("Year","Origin","Dest").filter(col("Year") == "2001"))
```

▶ (3) Spark Jobs

	Year	▲	Origin	▲	Dest	▲
1	2001		BWI		CLT	
2	2001		BWI		CLT	
3	2001		BWI		CLT	
4	2001		BWI		CLT	
5	2001		BWI		CLT	
6	2001		BWI		CLT	
7	2001		BWI		CLT	

Truncated results, showing first 1000 rows.

Figure 2.10 – Chaining and filtering with the filter method

> **Note**
>
> To browse through the complete list of functions in PySpark, check out the following link: `https://spark.apache.org/docs/2.4.0/api/python/pyspark.sql.html#module-pyspark.sql.functions`.

Dropping columns

To drop a column from a DataFrame, we use the `drop()` method. The syntax is as follows: `<dataframe>.drop(<column_name>)`. Run the following command:

```
airlines_1987_to_2008_drop_DayofMonth =  airlines_1987_to_2008.
drop("DayofMonth")
```

This will create a new DataFrame with the name `airlines_1987_to_2008_drop_ DayofMonth`, which will have all the columns from `airlines_1987_to_2008` except the `DayofMonth` column. Since this is a transformation, nothing really happens when we run this line of code.

Running `display(airlines_1987_to_2008_drop_DayofMonth)` will work as an action and trigger a Spark job:

```
1   # Create a new dataframe exluding dropped column
2   airlines_1987_to_2008_drop_DayofMonth = airlines_1987_to_2008.drop("DayofMonth")
3   # Display the new dataframe
4   display(airlines_1987_to_2008_drop_DayofMonth)
```

▶ (1) Spark Jobs

▶ ▦ airlines_1987_to_2008_drop_DayofMonth: pyspark.sql.dataframe.DataFrame = [Year: integer, Month: integer ... 26 more fields]

	Year ▲	Month ▲	DayOfWeek ▲	DepTime ▲	CRSDepTime ▲	ArrTime ▲	CRSArrTime ▲	UniqueCarrier ▲	FlightNum ▲	TailNum
1	1988	1	6	1348	1331	1458	1435	PI	942	NA
2	1988	1	7	1334	1331	1443	1435	PI	942	NA
3	1988	1	1	1446	1331	1553	1435	PI	942	NA
4	1988	1	2	1334	1331	1438	1435	PI	942	NA
5	1988	1	3	1341	1331	1503	1435	PI	942	NA
6	1988	1	4	1332	1331	1447	1435	PI	942	NA
7	1988	1	5	1331	1331	1434	1435	PI	942	NA

Showing the first 1000 rows.

Figure 2.11 – Dropping a column and creating a new DataFrame

Adding or replacing columns

We can use the `withColumn` method to add a new column or replace an existing column. We'll look at both of these instances. The syntax to add a new column is as follows:

```
<dataframe>.withColumn(<new_column>,<condition_or_
transformation>)
```

Running the following command will create a new column with a name of `Weekend`. It consists of a Boolean value where the `DayOfWeek` column is checked for values 6 and 7, using the `isin()` operator. If the `DayOfWeek` column equals 6 or 7, then we see `true`; otherwise, it will be `false`:

- Create the `Weekend` column and a new DataFrame:

```
AddNewColumn = (airlines_1987_to_2008
                .select('DayOfWeek')
                .withColumn("Weekend",col("DayOfWeek").
isin(6,7)))
```

- Display the new DataFrame:

```
display(AddNewColumn)
```

The preceding code block gives the following output in Databricks:

```
1   # Create column 'Weekend' and a new dataframe
2   AddNewColumn = (airlines_1987_to_2008
3                    .select('DayOfWeek')
4                    .withColumn("Weekend",col("DayOfWeek").isin(6,7)))
5   # Display the new dataframe
6   display(AddNewColumn)
```

▶ (1) Spark Jobs

▶ 🖿 AddNewColumn: pyspark.sql.dataframe.DataFrame = [DayOfWeek: integer, Weekend: boolean]

	DayOfWeek ▲	Weekend ▲
1	1	false
2	1	false
3	1	false
4	1	false
5	1	false
6	1	false
7	1	false

Truncated results, showing first 1000 rows.

Figure 2.12 – Adding a new column using the withColumn method

- Now, let's try replacing the values of an existing column. The syntax is almost identical to creating a new column:

```
<dataframe>.withColumn(<new_column>,<condition_or_
transformation>).
```

Run the following code block (cast the ActualElapsedTime column to an integer) and it will cast the ActualElapsedTime column from a string to an integer. We use the cast() function to change the data type of the column.

Although adding or replacing a column follows a similar syntax, logically, both are different operations on a DataFrame. When we use a column name that already exists in the DataFrame inside the withColumn clause, it will simply replace the existing contents of that particular column of the DataFrame.

- Cast the `ActualElapsedTime` column to an integer:

```
AddNewColumn = airlines_1987_to_2008.
withColumn("ActualElapsedTime",col("ActualElapsedTime").
cast("int"))
```

- Display the DataFrame:

```
display(AddNewColumn)
```

The output will not reflect any changes – but then, how do we check the data type of the column? Let's find out in the next section.

Printing schema

To print the schema of a DataFrame, we use the `printSchema()` function. The syntax is `<dataframe>.printSchema()`. Let's check the schema of the two DataFrames, `airlines_1987_to_2008` and `AddNewColumn`.

Run the following commands in two different cells:

- `airlines_1987_to_2008.printSchema()`
- `AddNewColumn.printSchema()`

Now, try to compare the outputs from the execution of the above commands. In the case of the `airlines_1987_to_2008` DataFrame, `ActualElapsedTime` has the data type of *string*. But for the `AddNewColumn` DataFrame, the same column has an integer data type.

> **Note**
> In the output of `printSchema()`, `(nullable = true)` simply means that the column accepts null values.

Renaming a column

The `withColumnRenamed` method is used to perform column renaming transformations. It returns a new DataFrame with the renamed column. The syntax is as follows:

```
<dataframe>.withColumnRenamed(<old_column_name>,<new_column_
name>)
```

Let's use the `AddNewColumn` DataFrame and rename the `DepTime` column to `DepartureTime`. Running the following command does the job for us:

1. Rename `DepTime` to `DepartureTime`:

```
RenameColumn = AddNewColumn.
withColumnRenamed("DepTime","DepartureTime")
```

2. Display the resulting DataFrame:

```
display(RenameColumn)
```

3. Here, we create a new Spark DataFrame, `RenameColumn`, with the column renamed:

```
1   # Rename 'DepTime' to 'DepartureTime'
2   RenameColumn = AddNewColumn.withColumnRenamed("DepTime","DepartureTime")
3   # Display the resulting dataframe
4   display(RenameColumn)
```

▶ (1) Spark Jobs

▶ 🖩 RenameColumn: pyspark.sql.dataframe.DataFrame = [Year: integer, Month: integer ... 27 more fields]

	Year ▲	Month ▲	DayofMonth ▲	DayOfWeek ▲	DepartureTime ▲	CRSDepTime ▲
1	1988	1	9	6	1348	1331
2	1988	1	10	7	1334	1331
3	1988	1	11	1	1446	1331
4	1988	1	12	2	1334	1331

Figure 2.13 – Renaming columns in Spark DataFrames

Dropping duplicate rows

Dealing with duplicate values is important when cleaning data. For this reason, Spark provides the `dropDuplicates` method. By default, it returns a DataFrame after dropping all duplicate rows. Optionally, we can define a subset of columns based on which of the rows get dropped. The syntax is as follows:

- Dropping all duplicate rows: `<dataframe>.dropDuplicates()`
- Dropping duplicate rows based on a subset of columns: `<dataframe>.dropDuplicates([<columns>])`

Let's try dropping rows from the `airlines_1987_to_2008` DataFrame. We will use the `Year` and `Month` columns as the subset to drop records. To do this, we can run the following lines of code:

- Drop rows based on `Year` and `Month`:

```
DropRows = airlines_1987_to_2008.
dropDuplicates(["Year","Month"])
```

- Display the DataFrame:

```
display(DropRows)
```

The code has only retained the unique combinations of the `Year` and `Month` columns and dropped all the other rows. The output is returned in the `DropRows` DataFrame:

```
1  # Drop rows based on Year and Month
2  DropRows = airlines_1987_to_2008.dropDuplicates(["Year","Month"])
3  # Display the dataframe
4  display(DropRows)
```

▸ (2) Spark Jobs

▸ 🗐 DropRows: pyspark.sql.dataframe.DataFrame = [Year: integer, Month: integer ... 27 more fields]

	Year	Month	DayofMonth	DayOfWeek	DepTime	CRSDepTime
1	1988	1	9	6	1348	1331
2	1989	1	23	1	1419	1230
3	1990	1	3	3	1707	1630

Figure 2.14 – Dropping rows using the dropDuplicates method

Limiting output rows

There may be times when we need not return all the rows from the DataFrame. To limit the number of rows returned, we can use the `limit()` method. The syntax for this is `<dataframe>.limit(<number_of_rows>)`. For instance, the `airlines_1987_to_2008.limit(10)` command returns only the top ten rows from the DataFrame. Enclosing it inside the `display()` function returns an output where we see only 10 records from the DataFrame:

```
display(airlines_1987_to_2008.limit(10))
```

Sorting rows

When a DataFrame needs sorting based on a particular column, we can use the `sort()` or `orderBy()` methods. The syntax for `sort()` is as follows:

- Sorting in an ascending order: `<dataframe>.sort(col(<column>).asc())`
- Sorting in a descending order: `<dataframe>.sort(col(<column>). desc())`

The syntax for `orderBy()` is identical. Let's use the `airlines_1987_to_2008` DataFrame and sort the rows by the `Year` column. Run the following blocks of code:

- Sort by descending order using `sort()`:

```
display(airlines_1987_to_2008.select("Year").
dropDuplicates().sort(col("Year").desc()))
```

This will give the following result:

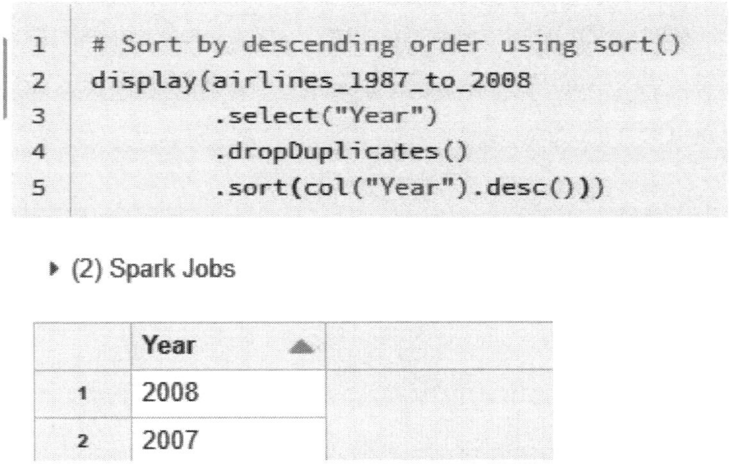

```
1   # Sort by descending order using sort()
2   display(airlines_1987_to_2008
3           .select("Year")
4           .dropDuplicates()
5           .sort(col("Year").desc()))
```

▸ (2) Spark Jobs

	Year ▲	
1	2008	
2	2007	

Figure 2.15 – Sorting the rows in a descending order

- Sort by an ascending order using `sort()`:

```
display(airlines_1987_to_2008.select("Year").
dropDuplicates().sort(col("Year").asc()))
```

This appears as follows in Databricks:

```
1   # Sorting by ascending order using sort()
2   display(airlines_1987_to_2008
3           .select("Year")
4           .dropDuplicates()
5           .sort(col("Year").asc()))
```

▶ (2) Spark Jobs

	Year ▲	
1	1987	
2	1988	

Figure 2.16 – Sorting in an ascending order

Next, let's see how to group data.

Grouping data

We can use the `groupBy()` method to group data and apply aggregate functions. This is often a very useful technique to analyze categorical data. The syntax to use `groupBy()` is `<dataframe>.groupBy().<aggregate_function>`.

Let's look at two examples using the `airlines_1987_to_2008` DataFrame:

1. We want to return a count of all the airports from where flights take off. We will do this by grouping our DataFrame with the `Origin` column and then return a count. Running the following command will do the job for us.

    Group data and return the value from the `count` function:

    ```
    display(airlines_1987_to_2008.groupBy("Origin").count())
    ```

This appears as follows in Databricks:

```
1   # Grouping data and returning count
2   display(airlines_1987_to_2008.groupBy("Origin").count())
```

▶ (2) Spark Jobs

	Origin ▲	count ▼
1	ORD	6597442
2	ATL	6100953
3	DFW	5710980

Figure 2.17 – Grouping data and returning a count value

2. We want to see the longest delay in arrival experienced by every destination airport. For this, we will group by the Dest column and find out the maximum value of the ArrDelay column.

    Grouping data and finding the maximum value for each Dest value:

    ```
    display(airlines_1987_to_2008.
    select(col("Dest"),col("ArrDelay").cast("int").
    alias("ArrDelay")).groupBy("Dest").max("ArrDelay"))
    ```

    This will give the following output:

```
1   # Grouping data and finding maximum value for each 'Dest'
2   display(airlines_1987_to_2008
3           .select(col("Dest"),col("ArrDelay").cast("int").alias("ArrDelay"))
4           .groupBy("Dest").max("ArrDelay"))
```

▶ (2) Spark Jobs

	Dest ▲	max(ArrDelay) ▲
1	MKC	12
2	BJI	96
3	RHI	175

Figure 2.18 – Grouping data and finding the maximum Dest value

> **Note**
>
> The `alias()` method is used to give a new name to the column while selecting or aggregating data.

We have learned about a lot of transformations so far! From selecting columns to performing aggregations, we've come a long way. But did you know that Databricks notebooks come with in-built data visualization capabilities? If you've already figured it out – amazing! But do not worry if you're haven't found out yet, as we'll cover that next.

Visualizing data

We will use the result obtained from the previous block of code, sort it in ascending order, and limit it to see the top 10 destination airports. Using the DataFrame returned, we'll create a bar chart:

```
# Visualizing data!
display(airlines_1987_to_2008         .select(col("Dest")
,col("ArrDelay").cast("int").alias("ArrDelay")).
groupBy("Dest").max("ArrDelay").limit(10))
```

This will give the following output:

▸ (2) Spark Jobs

	Dest ▲	max(ArrDelay) ▲
1	BGM	350
2	PSE	406
3	DLG	344
4	INL	175

Showing all 10 rows.

 Click to display visualization.

Figure 2.19 – Building visualizations in Databricks notebooks

The graph is shown in the following figure:

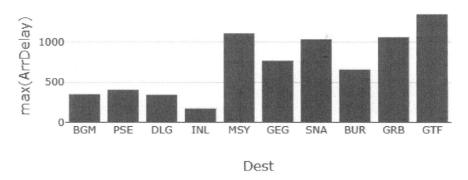

Figure 2.20 – Data displayed as a bar chart

> **Important Note**
> The visualization capabilities of Databricks notebooks are limited to a
> maximum of 1,000 records of any DataFrame. To plot visuals with larger
> datasets, we need to use specialized libraries or packages like **matplotlib**,
> **seaborn**, **ggplot2**, and more.

Writing data to a sink

Once we have performed transformations on the DataFrame, we can write it to our sink.
Or, in other words, save the transformed DataFrame. We will learn about writing data to
Delta Lake. Here, Delta Lake simply refers to writing data in our data lake in the open
source delta file format. The syntax for this is as follows:

```
<dataframe>.write.format('delta').option('path',<path_to_
load>).save()
```

Since we have already mounted our data lake on the Databricks workspace, we will use the
DBFS mount point to point to the data lake location. Our mount point's path is /mnt/
analyticsdatalakepackt_mnt.

Run the following code and replace the <mountpoint_path> section to write data into
Delta Lake:

```
AddNewColumn.write.format("delta").option("path","<mountpoint_
path>/transformed_data/").save()
```

Here, we are writing the `AddNewColumn` DataFrame to Delta Lake. The file created will have the name `transformed_data`. To confirm that the data has been successfully written, run the `%fs ls <path>` command in a new cell:

	path	▲	name
1	dbfs:/mnt/analyticsdatalakepackt_mnt/transformed_data/_delta_log/		_delta_log/
2	dbfs:/mnt/analyticsdatalakepackt_mnt/transformed_data/part-00000-552444cf-13a5-44a0-9eba-0369ac8f5fd0-c000.snappy.parquet		part-00000-552444cf-13a5-44a0-9eba-0369ac8f5
3	dbfs:/mnt/analyticsdatalakepackt_mnt/transformed_data/part-00001-e8a7e6fc-955d-4aeb-8f08-d8986c6b658c-c000.snappy.parquet		part-00001-e8a7e6fc-955d-4aeb-8f08-d8986c6b6
4	dbfs:/mnt/analyticsdatalakepackt_mnt/transformed_data/part-00002-f4276866-1ab4-4a9a-ae3a-d7b7468b6a97-c000.snappy.parquet		part-00002-f4276866-1ab4-4a9a-ae3a-d7b7468b
5	dbfs:/mnt/analyticsdatalakepackt_mnt/transformed_data/part-00003-9f75a5cc-816a-4f46-ac66-0cc828481937-c000.snappy.parquet		part-00003-9f75a5cc-816a-4f46-ac66-0cc828481
6	dbfs:/mnt/analyticsdatalakepackt_mnt/transformed_data/part-00004-31820c9b-eba0-4623-853d-07a0b708a4ac-c000.snappy.parquet		part-00004-31820c9b-eba0-4623-853d-07a0b708
	dbfs:/mnt/analyticsdatalakepackt_mnt/transformed_data/part-00005-f05dbb55-a9c7-4e95-9be8-ae32768ca799-		part-00005-f05dbb55-a9c7-4e95-9be8-ae32768c

Figure 2.21 – Viewing the contents of the Delta Lake file

With this, we have finished learning about various Spark transformations. Now, we will go through a worked-out example of an end-to-end batch ETL process.

Batch ETL process demo

Databricks professionals often talk about a **medallion architecture**. In this architecture, data processing in data pipelines is divided into three categories. We call them the *bronze*, *silver*, and *gold* layers. The bronze layer is often the raw data, the silver is the cleansed data, and the gold layer consists of aggregated or modeled data.

Check out `https://databricks.com/solutions/data-pipelines` for more information. In this section, we will walk through a real-world batch ETL process. We will perform the following steps:

- Read the data and create a Spark DataFrame.

- Perform transformations to clean the data and implement business logic.

- Write the DataFrame in the Delta Lake.

- Create a Delta table from written data and perform exploratory data analysis.

The dataset that we will be working with is part of `databricks-datasets` and located in the following directory:

```
dbfs:/databricks-datasets/samples/lending_club/parquet/
```

So, create a new **Python** notebook in Databricks, and let's get started:

1. Before we read the data, we will create a new `Hive` database. Our Delta table will be created in this database:

```sql
%sql
-- Create a new Hive database
CREATE DATABASE packt_databricks;
USE packt_databricks;
```

2. Read the data and create a Spark DataFrame. Note, that the data we are reading consists of five **Parquet** partition files. Extract or read the data by running the following code:

```
lending_club = spark.read.parquet("dbfs:/databricks-
datasets/samples/lending_club/parquet/")
```

3. Run the following command to view the first 10 rows of the DataFrame:

```
display(lending_club.limit(10))
```

4. Now it is time to perform transformations on the DataFrame. Here, we are selecting a subset of columns from the entire dataset, changing data types, and creating new columns:

```
from pyspark.sql.functions import *
```

I. The next block will select the columns that we are interested in:

```
lending_club = lending_club.select("loan_status", "int_
rate", "revol_util", "issue_d", "earliest_cr_line",
"emp_length", "verification_status", "total_pymnt",
"loan_amnt", "grade", "annual_inc", "dti", "addr_state",
"term", "home_ownership", "purpose", "application_type",
"delinq_2yrs", "total_acc")
```

II. This code transforms string columns into numeric columns using the `regexp_replace` and `substring` functions:

```
lending_club = (lending_club.withColumn('int_rate',
regexp_replace('int_rate', '%', '').cast('float'))
                        .withColumn('revol_util', regexp_
replace('revol_util', '%', '').cast('float'))
```

```
                           .withColumn('issue_year',
    substring(col("issue_d"), 5, 4).cast('double') )
                           .withColumn('earliest_year',
    substring(col("earliest_cr_line"), 5, 4).cast('double')))
```

III. Create the credit_length column:

```
lending_club = lending_club.withColumn('credit_length',
col("issue_year") - col("earliest_year"))
```

IV. Create the net column, which represents the total amount of money earned or lost per loan:

```
lending_club = lending_club.withColumn('net',
round(col("total_pymnt") - col("loan_amnt"), 2))
```

5. Write the data to Azure Data Lake Storage in Delta format. Replace the <mount_point> with the respective mount point:

```
lending_club.write.format("delta").save("dbfs:/
mnt/<mount_point>/lending_club_delta")
```

6. Create a Delta table in Databricks. Replace the <mount_point> with the respective mount point:

```
%sql
-- Create delta table in packt_databricks database
CREATE TABLE lending_club_delta
USING DELTA
LOCATION 'dbfs:/mnt/<mount_point>/lending_club_delta'
```

7. To confirm the creation of the Delta table in our database, packt_databricks, we can run the following command:

```
%sql
SHOW TABLES
```

8. Now, let's view the Delta table to view the first 10 records:

```
%sql
-- View the top rows from delta table
SELECT * FROM lending_club_delta LIMIT 10
```

9. To further explore the data, let's perform some queries. The first one is to understand the total *loan amount* that was given out for each *grade*. Once the DataFrame is returned, create a bar chart:

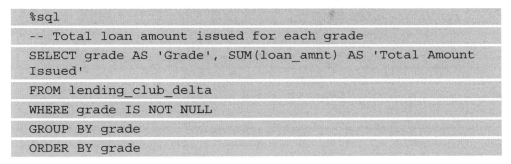

```
%sql
-- Total loan amount issued for each grade
SELECT grade AS 'Grade', SUM(loan_amnt) AS 'Total Amount
Issued'
FROM lending_club_delta
WHERE grade IS NOT NULL
GROUP BY grade
ORDER BY grade
```

The output is as follows:

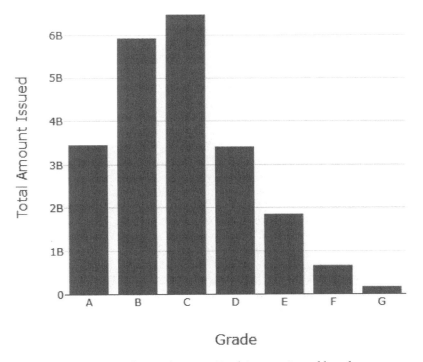

Figure 2.22 – The Grade versus Total Amount Issued bar chart

10. The second query that we'll run will return the *number of loans sanctioned* for every American *state*. Display a map visualization using the DataFrame:

```sql
%sql
-- Statewise distribution of loans
SELECT addr_state,
COUNT(*) AS 'Number of loans'
FROM lending_club_delta
WHERE addr_state != 'debt_consolidation'
AND addr_state != '531xx'
AND addr_state IS NOT NULL
GROUP BY addr_state
```

This gives us the following output:

Figure 2.23 – A map visualization in the Databricks notebook

This concludes our batch ETL demonstration. Now, let's move on to real-time processing in Databricks!

Learning Structured Streaming in Azure Databricks

Spark Structured Streaming provides a scalable and fault-tolerant approach to processing data in real-time. In Structured Streaming, Spark processes data in micro-batches to achieve low latencies. Syntactically, it looks very similar to batch processing. The same Spark DataFrame Transformations are used for streaming aggregations, joining static and streaming data, and more. Structured Streaming also guarantees **exactly-once stream processing**, which ensures that there is no duplication of data. Let's look at a quick example:

1. Create a new Databricks notebook, start your Spark cluster, and run the following command:

    ```
    %fs ls dbfs:/databricks-datasets/structured-streaming/
    events/
    ```

    This displays a list of 50 **JSON** files that we will be reading using Structured Streaming.

	path	name	size
1	dbfs:/databricks-datasets/structured-streaming/events/file-0.json	file-0.json	72530
2	dbfs:/databricks-datasets/structured-streaming/events/file-1.json	file-1.json	72961
3	dbfs:/databricks-datasets/structured-streaming/events/file-10.json	file-10.json	73025
4	dbfs:/databricks-datasets/structured-streaming/events/file-11.json	file-11.json	72999
5	dbfs:/databricks-datasets/structured-streaming/events/file-12.json	file-12.json	72987
6	dbfs:/databricks-datasets/structured-streaming/events/file-13.json	file-13.json	73006
7	dbfs:/databricks-datasets/structured-streaming/events/file-14.json	file-14.json	73003

Showing all 50 rows.

Figure 2.24 – Data to be read using Structured Streaming

2. Run the following code block. It imports the necessary functions, defines the schema for the DataFrame, and creates a streaming DataFrame. Note, the syntax is very similar to that of batch processing, where we use `.read` instead of `.readStream`. The `.option("maxFilesPerTrigger", 1)` means that every time our stream gets triggered, it will only process one file at a time. This means that our stream will be triggered 50 times and during every call, it will process one JSON file. In `.load()`, we have passed the location of the data:

    ```
    from pyspark.sql.functions import *
    ```

Define the schema for reading streaming:

```
schema = "time STRING, action STRING"
```

Create a streaming DataFrame:

```
stream_read = (spark
                .readStream
                .format("json")
                .schema(schema)
                .option("maxFilesPerTrigger", 1)
                .load("dbfs:/databricks-datasets/
structured-streaming/events/")
)
```

3. Once we have read the data, we will perform a transformation and then pass the DataFrame into the display() function:

```
stream_read = stream_read.withColumn("time",from_
unixtime(col("time")))
display(stream_read)
```

In this way, we can view the Spark DataFrame in real time!

▸ ⊘ display_query_8 (id: 2d3d9727-2a53-4826-8a3e-0a70ae434f8f)   *Last updated: 5 seconds ago*

	time	action
1	2016-07-26 02:45:07	Open
2	2016-07-26 02:45:47	Open
3	2016-07-26 02:46:42	Open
4	2016-07-26 02:46:59	Open
5	2016-07-26 02:47:05	Open
6	2016-07-26 02:47:14	Open
7	2016-07-26 02:47:25	Open

Showing the first 1000 rows.

Figure 2.25 – Displaying the Spark DataFrame in real time

4. Next, we will write the DataFrame to the Data Lake. This will also take place in real time! Run the following code block. Replace the `<mount_point>` with the respective mount point. The `checkpointLocation` ensures that our stream restarts from where it left off in case of an interruption. A path must be specified for the checkpointing as well.

The following code will write the stream to the Data Lake:

```
(stream_read
 .writeStream
 .format("delta")
 .option("checkpointLocation", "dbfs:/mnt/<mount_point>/
 write_stream_checkpointing")
 .start("dbfs:/mnt/<mount_point>/write_stream"))
```

5. Click on the green icon under **Spark Jobs**. This displays real-time graphs of the stream that we are running. These metrics are very helpful in understanding how the stream is performing:

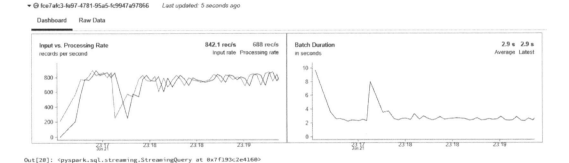

Figure 2.26 – Real-time metrics for Spark Structured Streaming in Databricks

6. Let's now create a Delta table using the data that is being written to the data lake. Run the following code block in a new cell. Make sure to replace the `<mount_point>` with the respective mount point:

```
%sql
CREATE TABLE stream_delta_table
USING DELTA
LOCATION 'dbfs:/mnt/<mount_point>/write_stream'
```

7.   Now, we can check the count of this Delta table. You will see that the count of the table returned increases every time the command is run. This means that our Delta table is being updated in real time using Structured Streaming:

```
%sql
SELECT COUNT(*) FROM stream_delta_table
```

Let's looks at some of the key concepts of Structured Streaming.

Structured Streaming concepts

In Spark Structured Streaming, the data is modeled as a continuous stream of appends to an unbounded table. Every append is treated as a micro-batch. This model allows data streams to get appended to a DataFrame as if it was a static input:

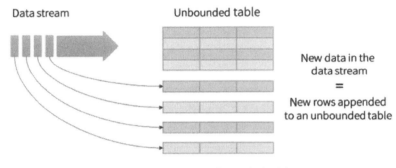

Figure 2.27 – How Spark Structured Streaming works

Structured Streaming also guarantees **exactly-once fault tolerance** with the help of **checkpointing** and **write-ahead logs** (**WALs**). At a high level, a structured stream tries to restart or reprocess the data in the event of a failure. This is benefitted by using sources that are repayable, like object storage and pub/sub messaging services. Examples of pub/sub messaging services include **Apache Kafka**, **Azure Event Hubs**, and more. Also, the streaming sinks are *idempotent* in nature, ensuring no data is written twice.

When reading the stream, the following should be taken into account:

- Every streaming DataFrame must have a schema defined. If the source system is a pub/sub messaging service, then the schema is automatically provided. In other scenarios, a schema should be defined manually.

- It is not advisable to infer the schema from files, as the number and size of these files will grow with time.

To create a streaming DataFrame, we use `.readStream` instead of `.read` as we would in a batch process or static DataFrames. Similarly, to write a stream, we use `.writeStream`, unlike a `.write` in a batch process.

> **Note**
>
> Just like in a batch process, data is only processed once an action is called on a streaming DataFrame. In the previous example, nothing actually happens when the `stream_read` DataFrame is created. The stream starts with Spark jobs only when the `display()` function is called.

Checkpointing helps to make Structured Streaming resistant to failures while writing data and provides exactly-once processing with Delta Lake. When using Azure Databricks, we define a checkpointing location either in **Azure Blob Storage** or Azure Data Lake. This location records the state of the stream as and when it progresses. This is very helpful in scenarios where our stream breaks and needs to be restarted. Upon restarting the stream, Spark will read the files in the checkpointing location. Then, it determines the most recent progress and resumes the stream from where it left off. The syntax to implement checkpointing is `.option("checkpointLocation", "<path>")`. Here, `<path>` is the location where the checkpointing logs will be written in Azure storage.

Streaming jobs that write data have several types of output modes. An **output mode** is simply the way our data gets written to a storage location using streaming. The following output modes are available:

- **Append**: The new rows added to the streaming DataFrame are written to the sink. The syntax is `.outputMode("append")`.
- **Complete**: The entire streaming DataFrame is written to the sink. The sink decides how this process is executed. The syntax is `.outputMode("complete")`.
- **Update**: Only the rows that got updated in the previous micro-batch are written to the sink. The syntax is `.outputMode("update")`.

Let's now look at examples of syntax differences between reading and writing a batch and a streaming process:

- Reading data in a *batch* process:

```
df = (spark
  .read
  .format("json")
```

```
    .schema(<schema>)
     .load(<path>)
  )
```

- Reading data in a *streaming* process:

```
df = (spark
  .readStream
  .format("json")
  .schema(<schema>)
   .load(<path>)
  )
```

- Writing data in a *batch* process:

```
(df
.write
.format("delta")
.mode("append")
.save(<path>))
```

- Writing data in a *streaming* process:

```
(df
.writeStream
.format("delta")
.option("checkpointLocation",<checkpointPath>)
.outputMode("append")
.start(<path>))
```

Triggers also play a crucial role in Structured Streaming. A trigger helps to define the time interval after which the next set of data is processed. When no trigger is specified, then the data is processed as soon as it arrives. Triggers are defined to determine how the micro-batches will be written to the sink. It is always recommended to use triggers when building Structured Streaming workloads. These include various categories:

- **Fixed interval**: A micro-batch is processed only after the fixed interval specified. The syntax is .trigger(Trigger.ProcessingTime("n minutes")). Here, n is the number of minutes.

- **One time**: The stream processes only one micro-batch and then automatically stops. The syntax is `.trigger(Trigger.Once())`.

- **Continuous**: This trigger is used to obtain streams of very low latency. The syntax is `.trigger(Trigger.Continuous("1 second"))`.

Managing streams

In production systems, several streams run simultaneously, and managing them well is of utmost importance. Hence, for our needs, there are several methods that can be called to manage these streams. Let's look again at the previous example and run this piece of code to write the stream to Azure Data Lake:

```
query = (stream_read
.writeStream
.format("delta")
.option("checkpointLocation", "dbfs:/write_stream_
checkpointing")
.start("dbfs:/write_stream"))
```

Here, we are creating a streaming object with the name `query`. Now, we will call the following methods on this object to further manage our stream:

- `query.id`: This returns the unique identifier of the running stream.

- `query.runId`: This returns the unique identifier of this run of the stream.

- `query.name`: This returns the name of the stream.

- `query.explain()`: This returns the physical query plan of the streaming job. The physical plan simply determines how the command will run on the Spark cluster.

- `query.stop()`: This stops a running streaming job.

- `query.recentProgress`: This returns an array of the most recent progress updates of the streaming query.

```
1   query.recentProgress
```

```
Out[17]: [{'id': '2ac9b765-5b39-4028-8715-f6d548a4f956',
 'runId': 'fca904d5-340a-4182-ac63-13dc20e8f13d',
 'name': None,
 'timestamp': '2021-06-23T17:37:55.604Z',
 'batchId': 18,
 'numInputRows': 2000,
 'inputRowsPerSecond': 600.0600060006001,
 'processedRowsPerSecond': 691.5629322268327,
 'durationMs': {'addBatch': 1944,
  'getBatch': 408,
  'latestOffset': 182,
  'queryPlanning': 7,
  'triggerExecution': 2892,
  'walCommit': 172},
 'stateOperators': [],
 'sources': [{'description': 'FileStreamSource[dbfs:/databricks-datasets/structured-streaming/events]',
  'startOffset': {'logOffset': 17},
  'endOffset': {'logOffset': 18},
  'numInputRows': 2000,
  'inputRowsPerSecond': 600.0600060006001,
  'processedRowsPerSecond': 691.5629322268327}],
```

Figure 2.28 – Using the .recentProgress method

- `query.lastProgress`: This returns the last progress of the streaming query.

```
1   query.lastProgress
```

```
Out[18]: {'id': '2ac9b765-5b39-4028-8715-f6d548a4f956',
 'runId': 'fca904d5-340a-4182-ac63-13dc20e8f13d',
 'name': None,
 'timestamp': '2021-06-23T17:51:25.000Z',
 'batchId': 50,
 'numInputRows': 0,
 'inputRowsPerSecond': 0.0,
 'processedRowsPerSecond': 0.0,
 'durationMs': {'latestOffset': 284, 'triggerExecution': 284},
 'stateOperators': [],
 'sources': [{'description': 'FileStreamSource[dbfs:/databricks-datasets/structured-streaming/events]',
  'startOffset': {'logOffset': 49},
  'endOffset': {'logOffset': 49},
  'numInputRows': 0,
  'inputRowsPerSecond': 0.0,
  'processedRowsPerSecond': 0.0}],
 'sink': {'description': 'DeltaSink[dbfs:/write_stream]', 'numOutputRows': -1}}
```

Figure 2.29 – Using the .lastProgress method

Next, we'll look at sorting our data.

Sorting data

Most operations performed on a streaming DataFrame are identical to those in batch or static DataFrames. One operation that is not possible is a sort on a streaming DataFrame. Since a streaming DataFrame is modeled as a continuous stream of appends to a table, it is just not feasible to sort this resulting table, because records keep getting added in real time.

Let's run the following code in a new cell. We will try to sort a streaming DataFrame by the `time` column, using a `try-catch` block to catch and print the exception:

```
try:
    (display(stream_read.sort(col("time").desc())))
except Exception as e:
    print(e)
```

Note the error that we get. It says, `Sorting is not supported on streaming DataFrames/Datasets, unless it is on aggregated DataFrame/ Dataset in Complete output mode;`.

We need to aggregate the data and use `.outputMode("complete")` to use the `sort` function.

Productionizing Structured Streaming

There are some key points to keep in mind when using Structured Streaming in a production environment:

- Checkpointing must be enabled for streams. This helps in case of failure, as the stream can then resume from where it left off.

- We can configure a Databricks job to run one or more streams in parallel. We can create a Databricks notebook and a schedule for it using Databricks jobs. Whenever a stream fails, Databricks will automatically terminate the complete job and restart all the streams in the notebook. This helps with automating recovery from failed stream jobs.

- **Watermarking** helps in dealing with data that arrives late. For instance, let's say we are aggregating a stream, but data starts arriving late. This will put pressure on Spark to process the late-arriving data, along with doing the aggregations. In this scenario, watermarking helps to set a definite time interval, beyond which late-arriving data is not considered for aggregations. The syntax for this is `.withWatermark("timestamp", "n minutes")`. If the watermark is set to be 20 minutes, then Spark will only tolerate late data for that time interval. Whatever data arrives for the batch after 20 minutes will not be included in the aggregation. Or, in other words, it may simply be dropped.

> **Note**
>
> To learn more about Spark Structured Streaming, check out the documentation: `https://spark.apache.org/docs/latest/structured-streaming-programming-guide.html`.

Summary

In this chapter, we learned about batch and stream processing. We started with the differences between the two processing paradigms and then progressed to mounting Azure storage on Databricks. This was followed by a deep dive into batch processing and Spark transformations. We also looked at a real-world example of a batch ETL process, where we read data in Parquet, transformed it, and wrote it back to Delta Lake.

Last but not the least, we also learned about Spark Structured Streaming, with an example. Spark Structured Streaming is ideal for reading and writing data in real time. Several downstream applications require real-time data, such as real-time dashboards.

In the next chapter, we will learn about machine learning and graph processing in Databricks. We will also go through plenty of examples to aid the learning process.

3
Learning about Machine Learning and Graph Processing in Databricks

Databricks is ideal for productionalizing data science projects. It provides specialized runtimes for **machine learning (ML)** and integration with **MLflow**. MLflow is an open source project that helps to manage an **end-to-end (E2E)** ML life cycle. Databricks provides a managed version of MLflow as part of its complete offering.

Graph processing is yet another offering in Databricks. This is made available by **GraphFrames**, a Spark package that makes graph analysis accessible using DataFrames. We will look at examples for both ML and graph processing in this chapter.

The following topics are covered in this chapter:

- Learning about ML components in Databricks
- Practicing ML in Databricks
- Learning about MLflow
- Learning about graph analysis in Databricks

Technical requirements

To follow the hands-on examples in the chapter, the following is required:

- An Azure subscription
- Azure Databricks
- Azure Databricks notebooks and a Spark cluster
- The following GitHub repository: `https://github.com/PacktPublishing/Optimizing-Databricks-Workload/tree/main/Chapter03`

Learning about ML components in Databricks

The Databricks workspace is broadly divided into two personas: **Data Science and Engineering** and **Machine Learning**. We've already looked at the **Data Science and Engineering** persona. In this chapter, we will understand and work with elements in the **Machine Learning** persona. This workspace persona consists of additional tabs in the left pane. These include **Experiments**, **Feature Store**, and **Models**. To switch to the **Machine Learning** workspace, click on **Data Science** and **Engineering** in the left pane and select **Machine Learning**. This brings up the new persona, as illustrated in the following screenshot:

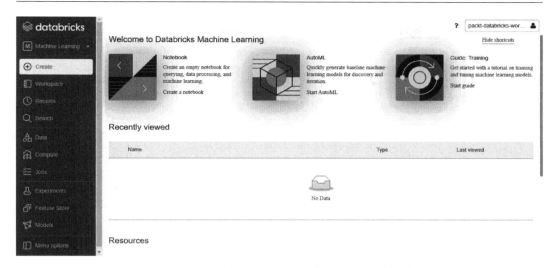

Figure 3.1 – Machine Learning workspace in Databricks

Let's now discuss the three most important elements of this workspace, as follows:

- **Experiments**: This section gives access to all the MLflow experiments across the workspace. We will work with this section once we start learning about MLflow.

- **Feature Store**: This is a collection of features stored in tables and converted from raw data. Teams often want to make use of features created and used by data scientists across an organization. This is made possible by the **Feature Store** in Databricks. It also allows you to create, reuse, and explore new features. These features can also be used for training and scoring ML models. The table-storing features are backed by Delta tables. Also, the Databricks runtime version required is 8.3 ML or above.

- **Models**: This section takes us to a repository of all the ML models created and tracked using MLflow. It also provides model lineage, versioning, and stage transitioning (moving a model from staging to production). In short, it provides the complete life cycle of the model. We will work with this section once we start learning about MLflow.

Next, we will go through an ML experiment using Spark ML in Azure Databricks.

Practicing ML in Databricks

In this section, we will perform a simple ML experiment in Databricks using Spark ML. We will begin with **exploratory data analysis** (**EDA**) to understand the dataset. Following this, an ML experiment using the **Decision tree** algorithm will be performed. Decision tree algorithms are usually used for classification problems.

We will be using data from the **DataSF** project that was launched in 2009 and contains hundreds of datasets from the city of San Francisco. The dataset we will be using concerns San Francisco's fire department. The dataset contains data about all the calls made to the fire department and their responses.

We will divide this section into three phases, as follows:

- **Environment setup**: Setting up a Spark cluster and getting the data
- **EDA**: Analyzing the dataset by answering questions to enhance data understanding
- **ML**: Using the Decision tree algorithm to address a classification problem

Environment setup

Let's start with the environment setup. Proceed as follows:

1. Spin up a new Spark cluster with the following configurations:

    I.   **Cluster Mode: Standard**

    II. **Databricks Runtime Version**: Runtime 8.3 ML (Scala 2.12, Spark 3.1.1), which is not a **graphics processing unit** (**GPU**)

    III. **Autoscaling**: Disabled

    IV. **Termination**: After 60 minutes

    V.   **Worker and Driver**: Standard_DS3_v2

    VI. **Workers**: 1

2. Next, we will create a new Python notebook, attach the cluster, and download the two datasets (in **comma-separated values** (**CSV**) format) in **Databricks File System** (**DBFS**). The following command downloads the first dataset using DataSF's **application programming interface** (**API**) in DBFS. Also, note that this is a large file and will take several minutes to download:

```sh
%sh
wget https://data.sfgov.org/api/views/nuek-vuh3/rows.
csv?accessType=DOWNLOAD -P /dbfs/firedata/dataset/
```

3. The following command renames the downloaded CSV file:

```
%fs
mv /firedata/dataset/rows.csv?accessType=DOWNLOAD /
firedata/dataset/Fire_Incidents.csv
```

4. The following command downloads the second CSV file into DBFS:

```
%sh
wget https://data.sfgov.org/api/views/wr8u-xric/rows.
csv?accessType=DOWNLOAD -P /dbfs/firedata/dataset/
```

5. The following command renames the second CSV file:

```
%fs
mv /firedata/dataset/rows.csv?accessType=DOWNLOAD /
firedata/dataset/Non_Medical_Incidents.csv
```

6. We can run the `%fs ls dbfs:/firedata/dataset/` command to confirm that our datasets have been downloaded into DBFS.

Next, let's move on to **EDA (Exploratory Data Analysis)**.

EDA

Let's start by reading the `Fire_Incidents` CSV file and creating a Spark DataFrame. Here are the steps for this:

1. The following code block manually defines the schema of the CSV file:

```
# Inferring the schema manually
from pyspark.sql.types import StructType, StructField,
IntegerType, StringType, BooleanType
manual_schema = StructType(
[
StructField('CallNumber', IntegerType(), True),
StructField('UnitID', StringType(), True),
StructField('IncidentNumber', IntegerType(), True),
StructField('CallType', StringType(), True),
StructField('CallDate', StringType(), True),
```

```
StructField('WatchDate', StringType(), True),
StructField('ReceivedDtTm', StringType(), True),
StructField('EntryDtTm', StringType(), True),
StructField('DispatchDtTm', StringType(), True),
StructField('ResponseDtTm', StringType(), True),
```

We will have to truncate the preceding code block. We encourage you to get the complete code block from the GitHub repository!

2. Now, we'll create a Spark DataFrame by reading the CSV file and passing the manually defined schema, as follows:

```
# Read the csv file as Spark dataframe but this time
using the manually defined schema
fire_incidents = (spark.read
                   .option("header",True)
                   .schema(manual_schema) # Use the schema
defined in previous cell
                   .csv("dbfs:/firedata/dataset/Fire_
Incidents.csv")
                   )
```

3. Let's look at the first 10 records of the DataFrame. The following command will do the job for us:

```
display(fire_incidents.limit(10))
```

We've now got our first DataFrame ready. Let's begin with the analysis! Here we go:

*   How many different types of calls were made to the fire department?

    Running the following code shows us the different types of calls that were made to the fire department. The category of call is specified using the CallType column:

    ```
    display(fire_incidents.groupBy("CallType").count())
    ```

*   How many years of fire service calls are present in the data?

Before we answer this question, let's take a look at the schema of the DataFrame using fire_incidents.printSchema(). Here, we can see that all the datetime columns are parsed as a string. We need to change this to timestamp.

We'll proceed as follows:

1. First, we need to enable Spark to overcome `SparkUpgradeException`. This arises due to a change in patterns of datetime strings between Spark 2.0 and Spark 3.0. The code to do this is shown here:

```
spark.conf.set("spark.sql.legacy.
timeParserPolicy","LEGACY")
```

2. Now, we will convert the data types of the datetime columns from `string` to `timestamp`. Run the following code:

```
from pyspark.sql.functions import *
from_pattern1 = 'MM/dd/yyyy'
from_pattern2 = 'MM/dd/yyyy hh:mm:ss aa'
fire_incidents = (fire_incidents
    .withColumn('CallDate', unix_timestamp(fire_
incidents['CallDate'], from_pattern1).cast("timestamp"))
    .withColumn('WatchDate', unix_timestamp(fire_
incidents['WatchDate'], from_pattern1).cast("timestamp"))
    .withColumn('ReceivedDtTm', unix_timestamp(fire_
incidents['ReceivedDtTm'], from_pattern2).
cast("timestamp"))
    .withColumn('EntryDtTm', unix_timestamp(fire_
incidents['EntryDtTm'], from_pattern2).cast("timestamp"))
    .withColumn('DispatchDtTm', unix_timestamp(fire_
incidents['DispatchDtTm'], from_pattern2).
cast("timestamp"))
    .withColumn('ResponseDtTm', unix_timestamp(fire_
incidents['ResponseDtTm'], from_pattern2).
cast("timestamp"))
    .withColumn('OnSceneDtTm', unix_timestamp(fire_
incidents['OnSceneDtTm'], from_pattern2).
cast("timestamp"))
    .withColumn('TransportDtTm', unix_timestamp(fire_
incidents['TransportDtTm'], from_pattern2).
cast("timestamp"))
    .withColumn('HospitalDtTm', unix_timestamp(fire_
incidents['HospitalDtTm'], from_pattern2).
cast("timestamp"))
    .withColumn('AvailableDtTm', unix_timestamp(fire_
incidents['AvailableDtTm'], from_pattern2).
cast("timestamp")))
```

Display the DataFrame to see the changes in data using `display(fire_incidents.limit(5))`.

3. Finally, it is time to answer the question. Run the following code to find out the years' worth of data that we are working with:

```
# Years worth of data present with us!
display(fire_incidents.select(year("CallDate").
alias('Year')).distinct())
```

Next, we will look at service calls made during the Christmas and New Year holiday week. We'll address the following questions:

*   How many service calls were logged between December 25 and December 31, 2019?

    Run the following code to return the total number of calls that were made to the fire department between December 25 and December 31:

```
# Number of service calls logged in between 25th Dec. to
31st Dec. 2019
fire_incidents.filter((year("CallDate") == 2019) &
(month("CallDate") == 12) & (dayofmonth("CallDate") >=
25)).count()
```

*   What is the distribution of service calls made between December 1, 2019 and January 1, 2020?

    Run the following code to understand the distribution of calls that were made to the fire department in this 1-month period:

```
# Line plot to showcase trend of service calls made
between 1st Dec. 2019 to 1st Jan. 2020
display(fire_incidents
        .filter((col("CallDate") >= '2019-12-01') &
(col("CallDate") < '2020-01-02'))
        .groupBy(col("CallDate").alias("Date"))
        .count()
        .orderBy(col("Date")))
```

Try creating a line plot from the result obtained to better understand the trend!

- What is the number of service calls made between December 25 and December 31 for the past 20 years?

Running the following code block helps us to understand the trend of service calls logged in between December 25 and December 31, from 2000 to 2020:

```
# Number of service calls logged in between 25th Dec. to
31st Dec. between 2000 and 2020
display(fire_incidents
        .filter((month("CallDate") == 12) &
(dayofmonth("CallDate") >= 25))
        .groupBy(year('CallDate').alias('Year'))
        .count()
        .orderBy('Year'))
```

- Which neighborhood generated the most calls last year?

To answer this question, let's switch from PySpark to Spark SQL. We will create a temporary view from the DataFrame and run a **Structured Query Language** (SQL) query, as follows:

```
# Create view to run the SQL syntax
fire_incidents.createOrReplaceTempView('fire_incidents_
view')
```

The following code runs the SQL query:

```
spark.sql("""SELECT NeighborhoodDistrict, COUNT(*) AS
Count
FROM fire_incidents_view
WHERE year(CallDate) = 2019
GROUP BY NeighborhoodDistrict
ORDER BY COUNT(1) DESC""")
```

Now, it's time for the final question!

- What was the primary non-medical reason most people called the fire department from Tenderloin last year during the Christmas holidays?

Before we answer this question, we need to read the second CSV file and create a Spark DataFrame.

The following code reads the second CSV file and renames the columns:

```
# Read the new csv file and rename column with spaces
non_medical_incidents = (spark.read
                         .option("header",True)
                         .option("inferSchema", True)
                         .csv("dbfs:/firedata/dataset/
Non_Medical_Incidents.csv")
                         .withColumnRenamed("Incident
Number","IncidentNumber")
                         .withColumnRenamed("Exposure
Number","ExposureNumber")
                         .withColumnRenamed("Incident
Date","IncidentDate")
                         .withColumnRenamed("Call
Number","CallNumber")
                         .withColumnRenamed("Alarm
DtTm","AlarmDtTm")
                         .withColumnRenamed("Arrival
DtTm","ArrivalDtTm")
                         .withColumnRenamed("Close
DtTm","CloseDtTm")
                         .withColumnRenamed("Station
Area","StationArea")
```

We will have to truncate the preceding code block. We encourage you to get the complete code block from the GitHub repository!

We can display the first three rows from the DataFrame to get a glimpse of the data. Run the following command to view the DataFrame:

```
display(non_medical_incidents.limit(3))
```

Next, we will join the `fire_incidents` and `non_medical_incidents` DataFrames. We will use the resulting joined DataFrame to answer the last question. Proceed as follows:

1. Run the following code to join the two DataFrames and drop duplicate columns:

```
# Join the two dataframes on the IncidentNumber column
joinedDF = (fire_incidents
            .join(non_medical_incidents,fire_incidents.
IncidentNumber == non_medical_incidents.IncidentNumber)
            .drop(non_medical_incidents.IncidentNumber)
```

```
                .drop(non_medical_incidents.City)
                .drop(non_medical_incidents.StationArea)
                .drop(non_medical_incidents.CallNumber)
                .drop(non_medical_incidents.Battalion)
                .drop(non_medical_incidents.
SupervisorDistrict)
                .drop(non_medical_incidents.NumberofAlarms)
                .drop(non_medical_incidents.Address)
                .drop(non_medical_incidents.Box))
```

2. Here, we create a new DataFrame, joinedDF, which is a result of joining
    fire_incidents and non_medical_incidents. Now, we will run the
    following command using joinedDF to give us the primary non-medical reasons
    for calling fire services in Tenderloin during 2019's Christmas holidays:

```
# Primary non-medical reasons for calling fire service in
Tenderloin during Christmas holidays last year
display(joinedDF
        .filter((col("CallDate") >= '2019-
12-24') & (col("CallDate") < '2020-01-02') &
(col('NeighborhoodDistrict') == 'Tenderloin'))
        .groupBy("PrimarySituation")
        .count()
        .orderBy(col('count').desc())
      )
```

Notice the first few records in the result displayed! With this, we conclude our EDA.

Let's now do some ML!

ML

Our ML scenario will involve predicting whether a fire incident requires **Advanced
Life Support** (**ALS**) or not. ALS is a special team of fire personnel deployed for critical
scenarios. The column we'll predict is ALSUnit, a Boolean column. We have selected
the following columns as features from the fire_incidents DataFrame as part of
our **feature engineering** (**FE**) process because they better represent the underlying
classification problem:

- CallType
- StationArea

- FinalPriority
- NumberofAlarms
- UnitType - Categorical
- ResponseDtTm (derived feature) = DispatchDtTm - ReceivedDtTm

Since we are dealing with a classification problem, we'll use the Decision tree algorithm for our use case. Decision tree algorithms are used largely for non-linear datasets to predict chance event outcomes, hence they are suitable for our classification problem use case. We'll proceed as follows:

1. First, we will import the required Spark ML libraries and algorithms. Run the following code to import all the necessary libraries and functions:

```
# Importing Libraries
from pyspark.ml import Pipeline
from pyspark.ml.feature import StringIndexer
from pyspark.ml.linalg import Vectors
from pyspark.ml.feature import VectorAssembler
from pyspark.ml.classification import
DecisionTreeClassifier
from pyspark.ml.evaluation import
MulticlassClassificationEvaluator
```

2. Now, we will select the feature columns and the target column and create the derived features, as follows:

```
# Selecting Feature columns and Target column
selectionDF = (
    fire_incidents.select("CallType","StationArea",
"FinalPriority","NumberofAlarms","UnitType",
"ReceivedDtTm","DispatchDtTm","ALSUnit")
    .withColumn("ResponseDtTm",unix_
timestamp("DispatchDtTm") - unix_
timestamp("ReceivedDtTm")) # In seconds
    .withColumn("StationArea",fire_incidents.StationArea.
cast(IntegerType()))
    .withColumn("ALSUnit",fire_incidents.ALSUnit.
cast(IntegerType()))
)
```

3. Display the resulting DataFrame using `display(selectionDF)`.

4. Next, we will split the DataFrame into `training` and `test` DataFrames. This helps us to prevent overfitting and at the same time test how the model is performing. Here's the code we'll need:

```
# Splitting the dataframe into training and test
dataframes
training = selectionDF.filter(year("DispatchDtTm")!=2018)
test = selectionDF.filter(year("DispatchDtTm")==2018)
```

5. Let's look at the number of records in the `training` and `test` DataFrames, as follows:

```
# Print the count of training and testing datasets
print(training.count(), test.count())
```

6. Now, we will train our ML model. The following code performs **feature transformations** (**FTs**), creates a pipeline, and trains a Decision tree algorithm on the `training` DataFrame.

`StringIndexer` converts a string column into a column of indices. `VectorAssembler` is a transformer that converts a given list of columns into a single vector column. `DecisionTreeClassifier` helps to train a Decision tree algorithm. `Pipeline` creates a ML pipeline that puts this series of activities in sequence. The code is illustrated in the following snippet:

```
# Model training
indexerCallType = StringIndexer(inputCol="CallType",
outputCol="CallTypeIndex", handleInvalid="skip")
indexerUnitType = StringIndexer(inputCol="UnitType",
outputCol="UnitTypeIndex", handleInvalid="skip")
assembler = VectorAssembler(
inputCols=["CallTypeIndex", "UnitTypeIndex",
"StationArea", "FinalPriority", "ResponseDtTm"],
    outputCol="features", handleInvalid="skip")
dt = DecisionTreeClassifier(maxDepth=3,
labelCol="ALSUnit", featuresCol="features")
pipeline = Pipeline(stages=[indexerCallType,
indexerUnitType, assembler, dt])
model = pipeline.fit(training)
```

Note the time taken to train the model on the 5-million-rows dataset!

7. Finally, it's time to make some predictions. Run `predictions = model.transform(test)` to make predictions on the `test` DataFrame. We can also display predictions for the first 1,000 records using `display(predictions.select("ALSUnit", "prediction"))`.

8. Last but not least, we will determine the accuracy of our ML model. Run the following command to check the accuracy of the model:

```
# Determine accuracy
evaluator = MulticlassClassificationEvaluator(
    labelCol="ALSUnit",
    predictionCol="prediction",
    metricName="accuracy")
accuracy = evaluator.evaluate(predictions)
print(accuracy)
```

Phew! That was quite some work. With this hands-on exercise, we have learned how to perform a simple ML experiment in Databricks. Next, we will learn about MLflow to manage the E2E ML life cycle.

Learning about MLflow

MLflow is an open source project from Databricks that helps to manage ML life cycles. Databricks provides a completely managed and hosted version of MLflow. The features of MLflow include the following:

- **Tracking**: Data scientists train several models at a time, and it can be hard to track them all. MLflow makes it easy to track the trained models using different algorithms, by providing a logging mechanism. We can even compare different results and parameters.

- **Artifacts**: The models can be packaged in reusable forms and shared with other data scientists and ML engineers.

- **Registering**: MLflow allows us to register different ML models and even different versions of these models. This makes it easy to manage an ML model's entire life cycle and allows for transitioning.

- **Deployment**: The models registered using MLflow can be hosted as **REpresentational State Transfer** (**REST**) endpoints. This allows for easy model querying and deployment.

MLflow tracking is built around the concept of **runs** and **experiments**. A run is simply data science and ML code that trains and tests a model. Several runs are aggregated under a common experiment, and MLflow consists of a server that can host several experiments.

MLflow tracking also helps to track, store, and deploy models into production. The experiments can be tracked using Python, R, Java, **command-line interface** (**CLI**), and REST API calls. Every run of an MLflow experiment helps to track the following:

- **Parameters**: Key-value pairs of model parameters
- **Metrics**: The metrics that help to evaluate a model, such as **Root Mean Square Error** (**RMSE**)
- **Artifacts**: Output files such as images and pickled models
- **Source**: The original code that ran the experiment

To better understand MLflow and its integral components, let's jump to another E2E example. In this worked-out example, we will be working with a bike rentals dataset. The rental process of sharing bikes depends highly on environmental and seasonal factors. The rental behaviors of consumers can be affected by factors such as precipitation and weather conditions. The dataset belongs to the Capital Bikeshare system, Washington D.C.

Here, we will be predicting bike rental count hourly based on the environmental and seasonal settings. The dataset is already available in DBFS as a CSV file and is located at `dbfs:/databricks-datasets/bikeSharing/data-001/hour.csv`. Spin up a Spark cluster, create a new notebook, and let's get started!

Spin up a new Spark cluster with the following configurations:

- **Cluster Mode**: **Standard**
- **Databricks Runtime Version**: `Runtime 8.3 ML (Scala 2.12, Spark 3.1.1)`, which is not a **graphics processing unit** (**GPU**)
- **Autoscaling**: Disabled
- **Termination**: After `60` minutes
- **Worker and Driver**: `Standard_DS3_v2`
- **Workers**: `1`

Once the cluster is active, we can start with the ML process! We'll proceed as follows:

1. First, it's time to import all the necessary libraries by running the following code:

```
# Importing necessary libraries
from pyspark.sql.functions import *
from pyspark.sql.types import *
import mlflow
import mlflow.spark
from pyspark.ml.regression import LinearRegression
from pyspark.ml.feature import RFormula
from pyspark.ml import Pipeline
from pyspark.ml.evaluation import RegressionEvaluator
from mlflow.tracking import MlflowClient
```

2. Next, let's get an understanding of the dataset. Run the following code: `%fs head dbfs:/databricks-datasets/bikeSharing/README.md`. This will print a **README** file giving details about the dataset.

3. We will now define the schema of the CSV file that we will be reading. Run the following code to manually define the schema:

```
bike_sharing_schema = StructType([
    StructField('instant',IntegerType(),False),
    StructField('dteday',StringType(),False),
    StructField('season',IntegerType(),False),
    StructField('yr',IntegerType(),False),
    StructField('mnth',IntegerType(),False),
    StructField('hr',IntegerType(),False),
    StructField('holiday',IntegerType(),False),
    StructField('weekday',IntegerType(),False),
    StructField('workingday',IntegerType(),False),
    StructField('weathersit',IntegerType(),False),
    StructField('temp',DoubleType(),False),
    StructField('atemp',DoubleType(),False),
    StructField('hum',DoubleType(),False),
    StructField('windspeed',DoubleType(),False),
    StructField('casual',IntegerType(),False),
    StructField('registered',IntegerType(),False),
```

```
    StructField('cnt',IntegerType(),False)
])
```

4. We will now read the CSV file and create a Spark DataFrame. Then, we will use the `display()` function to view the DataFrame. The code is illustrated in the following snippet:

```
bike_sharing = spark.read.option("header",True).
schema(bike_sharing_schema).csv("dbfs:/databricks-
datasets/bikeSharing/data-001/hour.csv")
# Display the dataframe
display(bike_sharing)
```

5. Let's now return the count of the DataFrame. Run `bike_sharing.count()`.

6. We will check the summary of the dataset. The `summary()` function helps to display metrics such as the count, mean, and standard deviation of the dataset. Run `display(bike_sharing.summary())` to display a summary of the dataset.

7. Next, let's begin with ML! We will split the DataFrame into `training` and `test` DataFrames. Run the following code to split the DataFrame and print the number of records in `training` and `test` DataFrames:

```
# Split the dataframe into test and train
(trainDF, testDF) = bike_sharing.randomSplit([.8, .2],
seed=42)
# Print the dataset in training and testing dataframe
print("# of records in training dataframe:",trainDF.
count())
print("# of records in testing dataset:",testDF.count())
```

8. Next, we will run a Python function that trains and tests a ML model, logs a tag, logs a parameter, logs the model, evaluates predictions, and logs the metric. The code is illustrated in the following snippet:

```
def ml_mlflow_register(run_name,formula,label,metric):
    """
    This function trains a linear regression model and
registers the model in the MLflow registry
    Argument:
    1. run_name - Name of the run
    2. formula - Formula for feature selection using
RFormula in the form 'label ~ feature1 + feature2'
```

```
    3. label - The column to predict
    4. metric - The metric to evaluate a model on
    """

    with mlflow.start_run(run_name=run_name) as run:
```

We will have to truncate the preceding code block. We encourage you to get the complete code block from the GitHub repository! Let's look at some of the important functions used in the preceding code block, as follows:

I.   RFormula: Helps to select features

II.   LinearRegression: Used for training a **linear regression** (**LR**) model

III. Pipeline: Creates an ML pipeline

IV.   mlflow.set_tag: Logs a tag using MLflow

V.   mlflow.log_param: Logs a parameter (here, the label column)

VI.   mlflow.spark.log_model: Logs the ML model being built

VII. RegressionEvaluator: Evaluates the LR model

VIII. mlflow.log_metric: Logs the metric used to evaluate the ML model

9. Now that we have a generic function ready to use MLflow tracking, let's call the function. We will call the function three times, each time using different arguments.

    For the first run, we will train the model using the temp and hum columns as features, as follows:

```
# First experiment run
ml_mlflow_register("first_temp_hum","cnt ~ temp +
hum","cnt","rmse")
```

    In the second run, we will build the model using the season, yr, mnth, hr, holiday, weekday, workingday, weathersit, temp, atemp, hum, and windspeed columns as features, as follows:

```
# Second experiment run
ml_mlflow_register("second_all","cnt ~ season + yr + mnth
+ hr + holiday + weekday + workingday + weathersit + temp
+ atemp + hum + windspeed","cnt","rmse")
```

In the third run, we will train the model using the `weathersit`, `temp`, `atemp`, `hum`, and `windspeed` columns, as follows:

```
# Third experiment run
ml_mlflow_register("second_only_weather","cnt ~ weathersit
+ temp + atemp + hum + windspeed","cnt","rmse")
```

The preceding code blocks trigger Spark jobs, and MLflow will record all the experiment runs.

10. Now, click on **Experiments** in the left-pane menu. This will open up a page where we can find all the experiments recorded for a notebook.

    We can see in the following screenshot that the name is `mlflow`. This is the name of the notebook. Here, you will see the name of your notebook. It is also the name of the experiment:

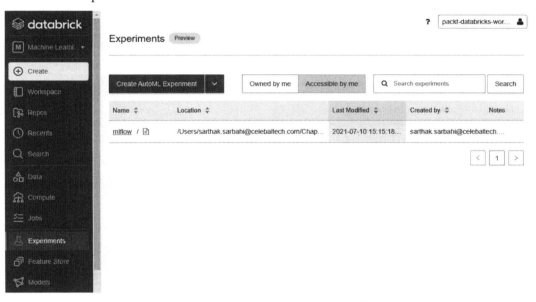

Figure 3.2 – Experiments in Databricks workspace

11. As a next step, click on the name of the experiment. This will take us to a page where we can find all the runs of the experiment, as illustrated in the following screenshot:

Figure 3.3 – Runs of the experiment

12. Let's click on the first run. This will take us to a new page where we can find the parameters, metrics, tags, and artifacts. Feel free to explore the different components on the page!

13. Now, under **Artifacts**, click on `model`. We will register this experiment run as a model. Click on **Register Model**. Click on **+ Create New Model**. Give a name to the model. The process is illustrated in the following screenshot:

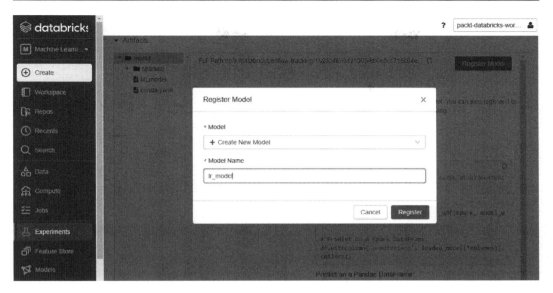

Figure 3.4 – Registering an experiment run as a model

14. Now, click on **Models** in the left menu. Here, we can find all the registered models, as illustrated in the following screenshot:

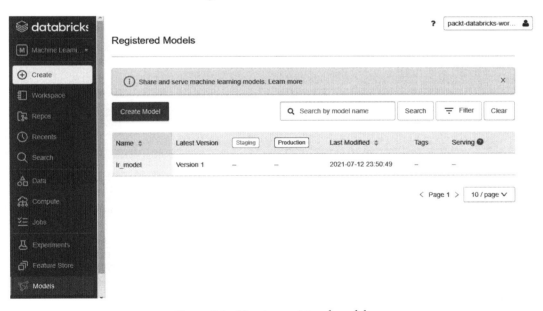

Figure 3.5 – Viewing registered models

15. Click on the registered model. Now, click on `Version 1`. Here, we can see that the **Stage** field for our model has been set to **None**. Let's suppose that we want to use this model for production. Click on **None** and select **Transition to -> Production**. Add a comment to describe the transition.

Congratulations! With this, we have successfully transitioned an experiment to serve as a production-scale ML model. We can also see in the following screenshot that the **Activities** section is updated with the transition:

Figure 3.6 – Stage transitioning in MLflow

16. It's time to head back to our notebook. We will now be querying our experiment runs' data. We will create a `mlflow_client_df` Spark DataFrame and then create a temporary view on top of it, as follows:

```
# Create a view to store metadata of all experiment runs
mlflow_client_df = spark.read.format("mlflow-
experiment").load()
mlflow_client_df.createOrReplaceTempView("my_experiment_
runs")
```

17. Now, let's query the temporary view. Run the following code. The `view` stores all the metadata about all the experiment runs. `artifcat_uri` is the endpoint that helps to instantiate the model. This means that the endpoint helps a developer to use the model for different applications:

```
%sql
-- View all runs
SELECT * FROM my_experiment_runs
```

18. Let's run another query using the view. This query returns the `experiment_id`, `run_id`, `start_time`, `end_time`, `metrics`, and `artifcat_uri` values of the different runs. The code is illustrated in the following snippet:

```
%sql
-- View experiment_id, run_id, start_time, end_time,
metrics, artifact_uri
SELECT experiment_id, run_id, start_time, end_time,
metrics.rmse as rmse, artifact_uri FROM my_experiment_
runs
```

With this, we conclude our MLflow example. In the next section, we will learn about graph processing and go through another example.

Learning about graph analysis in Databricks

Graph analysis is the study of graphs to help deliver actionable insights and make decisions based on relationships between entities. A graph is a visual depiction of data with vertices and edges that helps in establishing relationships between entities. Let's learn more about this with an example, as follows:

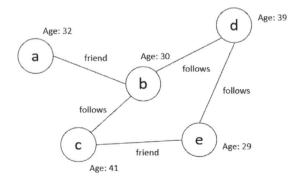

Figure 3.7 – An example of a graph

In the preceding screenshot, we can see an example of a typical graph. Here, the entities in the circles are called **vertices**. Each vertex is treated as an object that has its own properties called **attributes**. Every vertex has a relationship with another vertex in a graph. This is called an **edge**.

For instance, let's say vertex **a** represents a person named Mark and vertex **b** represents a person named Thomas. Mark has an attribute that states he is **32** years old. Similarly, Thomas is **30** years old. An edge between these two vertices states **friend**. This defines the relationship between the two—that is, of a friend. Similarly, let's say vertex **c** is Natasha and her age is **41**. Here, the relationship between Natasha and Thomas is that they follow each other on a social media platform.

This is also an example of a bidirectional relationship. There are also relationships that are unidirectional. For instance, say Natasha follows Thomas on social media but Thomas does not follow her back. This would be an example of a unidirectional relationship.

Now that we have a basic understanding of graphs, let's learn about some of the important concepts, as follows:

- **Total degree of a vertex**: The total number of edges that exist for a vertex.

- **Incoming and outgoing degree of a vertex**: When a vertex has an incoming relationship with another vertex, but it is not mutual—for example, say vertex **b** follows vertex **d** but vertex **d** only follows vertex **e**. In this scenario, the incoming degree of vertex **d** would be 1 (incoming from vertex **b**) and the outgoing degree of vertex **d** would be 1 (outgoing to vertex **e**).

- **Subgraph**: This is simply the subset of a larger graph. A subgraph has all its vertices and edges contained in a larger graph.

- **Breadth-first search** (**BFS**): BFS is an algorithm that is used to search for vertices in a graph. It is typically used to figure out if we can reach a given vertex from another vertex. We will use this algorithm in our worked-out example.

In Databricks, we use the **GraphFrames** package to perform graph processing or graph analysis. It provides APIs for both Python and Scala. Let's now start with our hands-on example!

Spin up a new Spark cluster with the following configurations:

- **Cluster Mode: Standard**

- **Databricks Runtime Version**: `Runtime 8.3 ML (Scala 2.12, Spark 3.1.1)`, which is not a **graphics processing unit (GPU)**

- **Autoscaling**: Disabled

- **Termination**: After 60 minutes
- **Worker and Driver**: Standard_DS3_v2
- **Workers**: 1

We will now begin with our example on graph analysis in Databricks. We'll proceed as follows:

1. Let's begin by importing the necessary libraries, like this:

    ```
    from pyspark.sql.functions import *
    from graphframes import *
    ```

2. Next, we will create a vertices DataFrame.

    Here, we will create a DataFrame with five columns. The id column will uniquely identify a record in the DataFrame. Every row pertains to a doctor, their age, their specialization, and the location of their practice. The code is illustrated in the following snippet:

    ```
    # Create vertices
    vertices = spark.createDataFrame([
        ("a", "Dr John", 54, "Cardiac Surgery", "Mumbai"),
        ("b", "Dr Nancy", 36, "Liver Transplant", "Mumbai"),
        ("c", "Dr Stark", 55, "Dentistry", "New Delhi"),
        ("d", "Dr Ross", 29, "Liver Transplant", "New Delhi"),
        ("e", "Dr Mensah", 32, "Dentistry", "New Delhi"),
        ("f", "Dr Brown", 36, "Cardiac Surgery", "New Delhi"),
        ("g", "Dr Ramish", 60, "Cardiac Surgery", "Mumbai")],
    ["id", "name", "age", "specialization", "location"])
    ```

3. Now, we will create an edges DataFrame.

    This DataFrame defines relationships between all the doctors in the vertices DataFrame. The src column defines the source vertex, the dst column defines the destination vertex, and the relationship column defines the edge between the two vertices. The code is illustrated in the following snippet:

    ```
    # Create edges
    edges = spark.createDataFrame([
        ("c", "d", "Work in CSM Hospital"),
        ("b", "c", "Attended New Delhi doctors conference"),
    ```

```
    ("c", "b", "Attended New Delhi doctors conference"),
    ("f", "c", "Friend"),
    ("e", "f", "Follows on Twitter"),
    ("c", "e", "Professor in college"),
    ("e", "c", "Student"),
    ("a", "g", "Cousin")
], ["src", "dst", "relationship"])
```

4. Create a graph from the `vertices` and `edges` DataFrames, as follows:

```
# Create a graph from vertices and edges
graph = GraphFrame(vertices, edges)
print(graph)
```

5. Let's display the `vertices` DataFrame using `display(graph.vertices)`.
    We can display the `edges` DataFrame using `display(graph.edges)`.

6. Let's now look at the incoming degree, outgoing degree, and degree of vertices, as follows:

    I.   Incoming degree: `display(graph.inDegrees)`

    II. Outgoing degree: `display(graph.outDegrees)`

    III. Degree of vertices: `display(graph.degrees)`

7. We will now run queries on the `vertices` DataFrame in the graph to analyze data, as follows:

    I.   Who is the youngest doctor among all the doctors in the graph?

    II. Here's the code you'll need for this:

```
# Youngest doctor
youngest_doctor = graph.vertices.groupBy().min("age")
display(youngest_doctor)
```

    III. How many doctors practice in Mumbai?

    IV. Here's the code you'll need for this:

```
doctors_in_mumbai = graph.vertices.filter(col("location")
== "Mumbai").count()
print(doctors_in_mumbai)
```

V. How many doctors are practicing dentistry in New Delhi?

VI. Here's the code you'll need for this:

```
dentistry_new_delhi = graph.vertices.
filter((col("location") == "New Delhi") &
(col("specialization") == "Dentistry")).count()
print(dentistry_new_delhi)
```

8. We will now run queries on the edges DataFrame in the graph to analyze data to find a count of relationships of those attending New Delhi's doctors' conference, as follows:

```
conference_count = graph.edges.filter(col("relationship")
== "Attended New Delhi doctors conference").count()
print(conference_count)
```

9. We will now build a subgraph to find any doctors who attended the conference or are older than 50 years, as follows:

```
subgraph = graph.filterEdges("relationship = 'Attended
New Delhi doctors conference'").filterVertices("age >
50")
display(subgraph.vertices)
```

10. Last but not least, we will use the BFS algorithm to search for doctors starting from Dr Brown with an age greater than 40 years.

Here, we start from vertex f (Dr Brown) and search for the next doctor who is older than 40 years:

```
# Search from Dr Brown for doctors with age > 40
display(graph.bfs("name = 'Dr Brown'","age > 40"))
```

This brings us to the end of our example using GraphFrames. This was just scratching the surface. To learn more, check out the documentation at https://graphframes.github.io/graphframes/docs/_site/user-guide.html.

Summary

In this chapter, we learned about ML and graph analysis in Databricks. We started with differentiating workspace personas for data engineering and ML. Following this, we went through an E2E example of ML, starting with EDA and ending with making predictions with the ML model. Next, we learned about MLflow with a worked-out example. In the later part of the chapter, we had a glimpse of the basic concepts of graph analysis and performed another hands-on tutorial.

Both ML and graph analysis help organizations build better products by solving exciting problems. But the major roadblock here is to practice it with big data. This is where Databricks changes the game completely!

In the next chapter, we will learn how to effectively manage Spark clusters. We will dive deeper into the details of when to use a particular kind of cluster. We will also learn about using Databricks pools, spot instances, and some important components of the Spark **user interface** (**UI**).

Section 2: Optimization Techniques

In this section, we learn how to optimize our Spark workloads in Databricks to increase performance and get real value out of Spark.

This section comprises the following chapters:

- *Chapter 4, Managing Spark Clusters*
- *Chapter 5, Big Data Analytics*
- *Chapter 6, Databricks Delta Lake*
- *Chapter 7, Spark Core*

4
Managing Spark Clusters

A **Spark cluster** in **Azure Databricks** is probably the most important entity in the service. Although it is managed for us from the infrastructure end, we must understand the right cluster setting for an environment.

In this chapter, we will learn about the best practices to manage our Spark clusters to optimize our workloads. We will also learn about the Databricks managed resource group, which will help us understand how Azure Databricks is provisioned.

We will learn how to optimize costs associated with Spark clusters with **pools** and **spot instances**. In the end, we will learn about the essential components of the **Spark UI** that can help us debug and optimize queries.

In this chapter, we will cover the following topics:

- Designing Spark clusters
- Learning about Databricks managed resource groups
- Learning about Databricks Pools
- Using spot instances
- Following the Spark UI

Technical requirements

To follow the hands-on tutorials in the chapter, you will need the following:

- An Azure subscription
- Azure Databricks
- Azure Databricks notebooks and a Spark cluster

Code samples from `https://github.com/PacktPublishing/Optimizing-Databricks-Workload/tree/main/Chapter04`

Designing Spark clusters

Designing a Spark cluster essentially means choosing the configurations for the cluster. Spark clusters in Databricks can be designed using the *Compute* section. Determining the right cluster configuration is very important for managing costs and data for different types of workloads. For example, a cluster that's used concurrently by several data analysts might not be a good fit for structured streaming or machine learning workloads. Before we decide on a Spark cluster configuration, several questions need to be asked:

- Who will be the primary user of the cluster? It could be a data engineer, data scientist, data analyst, or machine learning engineer.
- What kind of workloads run on the cluster? It could be an **Extract, Transform, and Load** (**ETL**) process for a data engineer or exploratory data analysis for a data scientist. An ETL process could also be further divided into batch and streaming workloads.
- What is the **service-level agreement** (**SLA**) that needs to be met for the organization using Databricks to build an enterprise data platform?
- What are the constraints on budget and cost for the workloads?

In this section, we will learn about various parameters, based on which an informed decision can be made to decide on the correct Spark cluster configuration.

Understanding cluster types

Spark clusters are broadly categorized into **all-purpose** and **job clusters**. All-purpose clusters can be used for several purposes such as **ad hoc analysis**, **data engineering development**, and **data exploration**. On the other hand, job clusters are spawned to perform a particular workload (an ETL process and more) and are automatically terminated as soon as the job finishes.

The best practice here is to do the development work using an all-purpose cluster and when the development needs to be run in production, a job cluster should be used. Doing this ensures that a production job does not unnecessarily keep a Spark cluster active, thereby reducing usage and cost.

Regarding cluster modes, there are three types available for all-purpose clusters:

- **Standard**: This mode is the most frequently used by users. They work well to process big data in parallel but are not well suited for sharing with a large number of users concurrently.

- **Single Node**: Here, a cluster with only a driver and no workers is spawned. A single-node cluster is used for smaller workloads or use cases, wherein data needs to be processed in a non-distributed fashion.

- **High Concurrency**: As the name suggests, a high concurrency cluster is ideal for use among many users at the same time. It is ideal for ad hoc analytical use cases. It is also recommended to enable autoscaling when using a high concurrency cluster.

The following screenshot shows the three types of cluster modes in Azure Databricks:

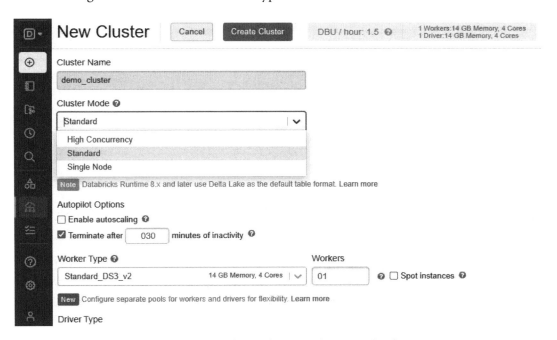

Figure 4.1 – Different cluster modes in Databricks

Next, we will learn about spot instances and how they are different to regular on-demand instances.

Learning about spot instances

So far, the cluster instances that we've discussed are on-demand instances. This means that both the driver and worker nodes are spawned when needed and are released when they're not in use (that is, when the cluster terminates). Apart from on-demand instances, there is another category called **spot instances**. Spot instances in Azure Databricks leverage **Azure Spot VMs**. Azure Spot VMs tend to be cheaper than on-demand instances as they provide unused capacities across the Azure infrastructure. This is the primary reason why they are so cost-effective.

But there's a tradeoff. The spot instances in a Databricks cluster can be evicted at any time with short notice from Azure. Nevertheless, this does not disrupt the existing Spark jobs as the evicted spot instances are automatically replaced by on-demand instances. Hence, spot instances are ideal for workloads in Databricks that can tolerate interruptions (preferably batch processes) and latency in compute. We will look at a quick tutorial on spot instances later in this chapter in the *Using spot instances* section.

> **Note**
> The discounts that come with spot instances vary across regions and also depend on Azure's available infrastructure capacity at the time of workload deployment in Databricks.

Learning about autoscaling in Spark clusters

Autoscaling means automatically scaling cluster worker nodes via Databricks. Autoscaling helps resize clusters (increase or decrease worker nodes) based on workloads. For example, say a cluster with autoscaling enabled has been instantiated with a minimum of two and a maximum of five worker nodes. Naturally, the cluster will start functioning with two worker nodes and as the processing load on the cluster increases, it will automatically scale up to increase the number of worker nodes. Although it takes some time for the cluster to scale up, autoscaling is greatly beneficial for lowering costs:

- Compared to a fixed-size cluster (no autoscaling), a cluster with autoscaling enabled only brings on new node instances where there is an actual need. This helps reduce costs.

- At times, it is difficult to decide on the cluster's size before running Spark jobs. Hence, there are chances that a cluster can get under-provisioned. Scaling up such a cluster can take more time and manual effort as somebody needs to edit the cluster configuration and then restart it. In such scenarios, autoscaling helps save a lot of time and effort.

- While running ETL workloads, it is possible to determine a cluster's size if the job remains the same over time. But if the data size increases unexpectedly, it is better to use autoscaling. Also, for long-running Spark jobs, autoscaling can be beneficial as there might be a time where the cluster might remain idle or may be under-utilized. At such times, autoscaling can help reduce a cluster's size, thereby lowering costs.

- There is also support for *autoscaling local storage*. This means that Databricks keeps an eye on disk space utilization across the cluster worker nodes. When a worker starts running low on the amount of free disk space, Databricks automatically provides an additional managed disk.

Next, we will provide a brief introduction to Databricks Pools.

Introducing Databricks Pools

Pools in Databricks are a set of ready-to-use node instances for the cluster. While creating a cluster, it can be attached to a pool, where it will pick instances directly from the pool. This leads to a reduction in cluster start times. When a cluster is terminated, the instances are returned to the pool and can be reused by any other cluster.

Databricks does not charge for DBUs when the instances are idle in the pool. Charges are only applied by the instance provider; that is, Azure. Pools are a great way to minimize processing time as cluster startup time reduces drastically. We will learn about Databricks Pools in depth later in this chapter.

Learning about Databricks runtime versions (DBRs)

The recommendations for **DBR** versions vary between use cases. The general recommendations are as follows:

- Databricks recommends that you use the latest DBR version for all-purpose clusters. The most recent versions provide the latest Spark optimizations and compatibilities.

- For job clusters, it is recommended to use the **long-term support** (**LTS**) Databricks runtime versions. The LTR versions prevent any compatibility issues.

- For use cases involving machine learning or genomics, it is recommended to use the specialized machine learning Databricks runtime versions.

The following screenshot shows the different Databricks runtime versions that are available:

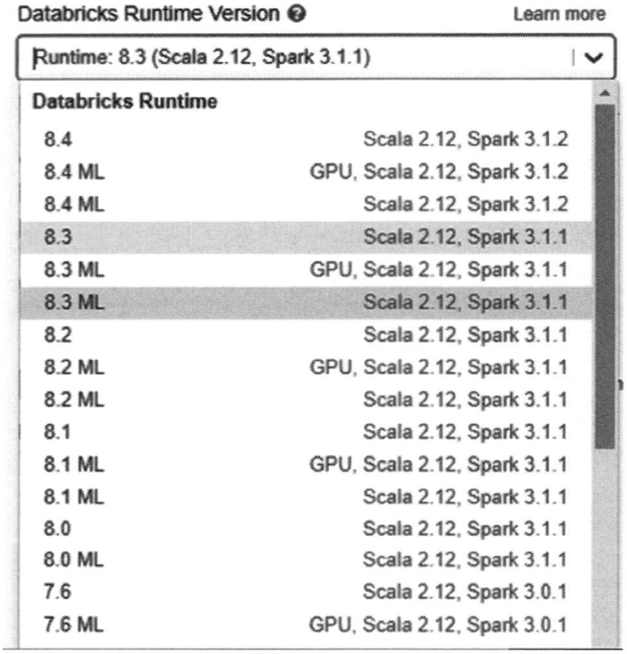

Figure 4.2 – Different DBRs available

Next, we will learn about the automatic termination feature in Databricks and how it is useful.

Learning about automatic termination

While creating a new cluster in Databricks, we get the option to specify the auto-termination time limit. This time limit ensures that the cluster automatically terminates due to inactivity. By default, this limit is set to *120 minutes*. Decreasing this limit can help reduce costs as DBUs keep getting charged even when the cluster is inactive before being terminated.

But it is also important to remember that when a cluster is terminated, its entire state is lost. This includes variables, temporary views, caches, and more. So, make sure the automatic termination limit is set in such a way that it does not hinder a developer's ongoing project.

> **Note**
> We will talk about caching in detail in the upcoming chapters when we start discussing optimizing techniques in Databricks.

Learning about cluster sizing

Most people think that deciding on a **cluster size** only means determining the number of workers for a workload. But this is not usually the case. When considering a cluster size, the following parameters should also be kept in mind:

- *The total number of cores in the cluster*: This is the maximum level of parallelism that a cluster can achieve.

- *The total memory or RAM in the cluster*: Since a lot of data is cached while processing Spark jobs, considering memory is also very important while designing a cluster.

- *Total executor local storage*: Local storage in executors store data when it gets spilled due to shuffling or caching.

Now, we will go through some cluster sizing examples, along with recommendations. This will give us an understanding of what to go for in what kind of a scenario.

Designing a Spark cluster for data analytics

Data analytical use cases involve slicing and dicing data to gather insights or prepare data for reporting. By their very nature, there may be several join operations (wide transformations), which leads to data shuffling across worker nodes. For data analytical use cases, the recommendations are as follows:

- Choosing a cluster with a fewer number of nodes is beneficial as it reduces the disk and network I/O needed to perform data shuffling.

- Automatic termination should be enabled to terminate the cluster in case of inactivity to reduce costs.

- Autoscaling must be enabled as per the analysts' workloads.

- High concurrency mode clusters can be used, considering there would be multiple analysts querying the data at the same time.

- Pools can be used to ensure consistent cluster configurations.

Now, let's look at the cluster sizing considerations for a simple batch ETL process.

Designing a Spark cluster for a simple batch ETL process

A **simple batch ETL process** involves reading the data from a source, performing minimal transformations, and loading it to a destination. Shuffling does not usually occur for simple batch ETL processes. The recommendations are as follows:

- Compute-optimized clusters, which are clusters with high numbers of cores, should be chosen as memory or local disk storage might not be required in large numbers.
- Pools can help reduce the total job runtime as the cluster startup time is decreased when using an all-purpose cluster.
- Job clusters must be used to productionize such workloads.

Now, let's look at the cluster sizing considerations for a complex batch ETL process.

Designing a Spark cluster for a complex batch ETL process

In a **complex batch ETL process,** data can be joined or a union can be created across multiple tables. In such scenarios, shuffling can be expected. The recommendations for a complex batch ETL process are as follows:

- A compute-optimized cluster with as few worker nodes as possible. This will ensure more parallelism and less network overhead costs.
- Pools can help reduce the total job runtime as the cluster startup time is decreased when using an all-purpose cluster.
- Job clusters must be used to productionize such workloads.

Now, let's look at the cluster sizing considerations for a streaming ETL process.

Designing a Spark cluster for a streaming ETL process

In a **streaming ETL** process, we would be reading real-time data in the form of events from data ingestion services or frameworks. The data is then transformed on the fly and written to data sinks. For example, real-time data from Azure Events can be read in Azure Databricks, transformed using Spark DataFrames, and written to a sink such as **Azure Data Lake Storage**. The recommendations for a streaming ETL process are as follows:

- A compute-optimized cluster must be used to ensure more parallelism.
- Pools can help reduce the total job runtime as the cluster startup time is decreased when using an all-purpose cluster.
- Job clusters must be used to productionize such workloads.

Now, let's look at the cluster sizing considerations for a machine learning use workload.

Designing a Spark cluster for machine learning workloads

Machine learning workloads often require storing all the training data in memory. This requires a lot memory or RAM in the cluster. The recommendations for machine learning workloads are as follows:

- A memory-optimized cluster must be used that accounts for enough RAM for storing large datasets in memory for effective model training.

- Choosing a cluster with a fewer number of nodes is beneficial as it reduces the disk and network I/O needed to perform data shuffling.

- Automatic termination should be enabled to reduce costs.

- If the storage and compute capacities are not enough for the workloads, consider using GPU-enabled instances.

This concludes our look at designing new clusters. Deciding on the correct Spark cluster configuration for the workloads is crucial to run jobs in an optimized fashion and at the same time, save costs. Everything we have learned in this section will provide us with the wisdom to make the correct decisions while creating our next Databricks cluster.

Learning about Databricks managed resource groups

In this section, we will take a look at the managed resource group of a Databricks workspace. A **managed resource group** is a resource group that is automatically created by Azure when a Databricks workspace is created.

In the majority of cases, we do not need to do anything in a managed resource group. However, it is helpful to know the components that are created inside the managed resource group of an Azure Databricks workspace. This helps us understand how the Databricks workspace is functioning under the hood.

To start, let's create a new cluster with the following configuration:

- **Cluster Mode**: **Standard**
- **Databricks Runtime Version**: `8.3 (includes Apache Spark 3.1.1 and Scala 2.12)`
- Autoscaling: Disabled

- Automatic termination: After 30 minutes of inactivity
- **Worker Type**: Standard_DS3_v2
- Number of workers: 1
- **Driver Type**: Same as the worker

Let's wait for the cluster to spin up and don't forget to give it a suitable name! We have created a cluster called new_cluster.

The managed resource group will be relevant again when we will learn about spot instances. The following screenshot shows that a new cluster has been created:

Figure 4.3 – A new cluster in Azure Databricks

Now, we can head back to the page from where we can launch our Databricks workspace. Here, we need to click on the link next to **Managed Resource Group**:

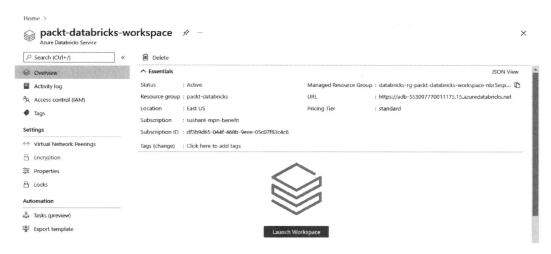

Figure 4.4 – Azure Databricks page for launching workspaces

This takes us to the managed resource group of the Databricks workspace:

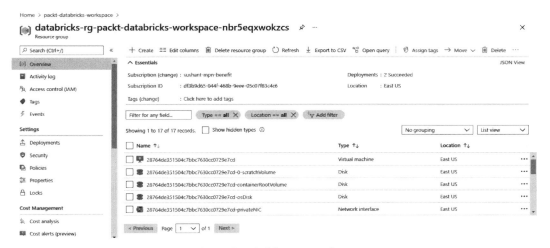

Figure 4.5 – Azure Databricks managed resource group

The managed resource group consists of several Azure services. Let's take a look at the most important resources:

- **Storage account**: This is the storage account that hosts all the data stored in the **Databricks File System** (**DBFS**).

- **Virtual machine**: These VMs run the Spark programs. The cluster that we see in Databricks consists of nodes and these nodes are backed by **Azure Virtual Machines**. Here, we can find two virtual machines: one for the driver and another for the worker. This is because we have created a two-node cluster. If there were more workers, we would have found that there are as many VMs in the managed resource group.

- **Virtual network**: **Azure Virtual Networks**, also called **VNets**, provides Databricks with a private network. This ensures that all the Azure resources concerning the Databricks workspace interact with each other in a secure fashion.

- **Network security group**: An **Azure Network Security Group** helps filter out network traffic from Azure resources that are part of a virtual network.

The Azure resources remain intact in the managed resource group, so long as the cluster is running. If the cluster is terminated or deleted from the Databricks workspace, all the Azure resources related to the Spark cluster are removed. These include VMs, disks, network interfaces, and public IP addresses.

Now, let's terminate the cluster and wait for a few minutes. After a while, we will see that the managed resource group will only be left with three Azure resources. This means that every time we spin a new Spark cluster, Azure provides fresh infrastructure resources for it.

The following screenshot shows that we are left with only three Azure resources since the cluster has been terminated:

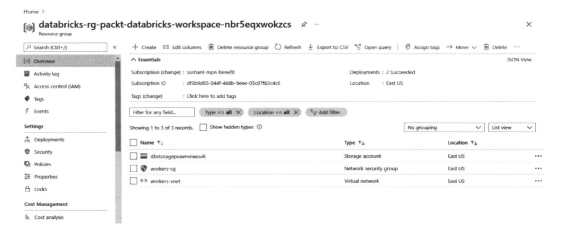

Figure 4.6 – Azure Databricks managed resource group

This wraps up our learning regarding managed resource groups. Next, we will set up our first Databricks pool!

Learning about Databricks Pools

In this section, we will dive deeper into Azure Databricks Pools. We will start by creating a pool, attaching a cluster to a pool, and then learning about the best practices when using Pools in Azure Databricks.

Creating a pool

To create a pool, head over to the Databricks workspace. Then, click on **Compute**, select **Pools**, and click on + **Create Pool**. This will open a page where we need to define the pool's configuration, as shown in the following screenshot:

Figure 4.7 – Creating a pool in Azure Databricks

Let's discuss the configurations one by one:

- **Name**: We need to give the pool a suitable name.

- **Min Idle**: This defines the minimum number of idle instances that will be contained in the pool at any given time. These instances do not terminate and when consumed by a cluster, they will be replaced by another set of idle instances.

- **Max Capacity**: This defines the maximum number of instances that can be present in the pool at any given time. It is an optional field but when set, it takes into account both the idle and used instances. If a cluster using the pool requests for more instances from the pool, that request will automatically fail. The *error* that will be thrown will be **INSTANCE_POOL_MAX_CAPACITY_FAILURE**. Azure Databricks recommends only setting a value for **Max Capacity** when the cost being incurred from the Pools must be capped.

- **Idle Instance Auto Termination**: This defines the time wherein the instances in the pool (above the **Min Idle** limit) will get terminated by the pool when idle.

- **Instance Type**: A pool's instance type defines the type of instance nodes that will be provisioned in the pool. The instance type remains the same for both drivers and workers. This means that even if the cluster takes instances for the driver or worker from the pool, the instance type is going to remain the same.

- **Preloaded Databricks Runtime Version**: This helps speed up the cluster's launch time using idle instances from the pool. When a cluster is created with the same DBR version as the preloaded DBR, the cluster launches even quicker.

- **Tags**: Pool tags help monitor the costs of the different resources that are part of the Azure environment. These tags are applied as key-value pairs of Azure's resources, such as virtual machines and disks.

- **All Spot**: To save costs, pool instances can be defined as spot instances as opposed to the default on-demand instances. In this case, the driver and worker instances from the pool will be provisioned as spot instances in the cluster.

Let's create a pool with the following configuration:

- **Name**: new_pool
- **Min Idle**: 1
- **Max Capacity**: 3
- **Idle Instance Auto Termination**: 30
- **Instance Type**: Standard_DS3_v2

- **Preloaded Databricks Runtime Version**: `Runtime: 8.3 (Scala 2.12, Spark 3.1.1)`
- **On-demand/Spot**: All on-demand

After waiting for a couple of minutes, we will see that the pool has provisioned one instance.

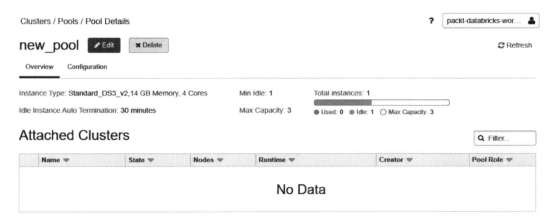

Figure 4.8 – Creating a pool in Azure Databricks

Now that we have covered how to create a Pool, let's attach a cluster to the Pool.

Attaching a cluster to the Pool

We will now attach a cluster to the **new_pool** pool that we in the previous section, *Creating a Pool*. Let's go back to **Compute** and create a new cluster. Create the following configuration for the cluster:

- **Cluster Name**: `DB_cluster_with_pool`
- **Cluster Mode**: **Standard**
- **Databricks Runtime Version**: `Runtime: 8.3 (Scala 2.12, Spark 3.1.1)`
- **Autoscaling**: Disabled
- **Automatic Termination**: After `30` minutes
- **Worker Type**: `new_pool`
- **Driver Type**: `new_pool`
- **Number of workers**: `1`

As shown in the following screenshot, our newly created pool is available as an option for both **Worker Type** and **Driver Type** while setting the cluster configuration:

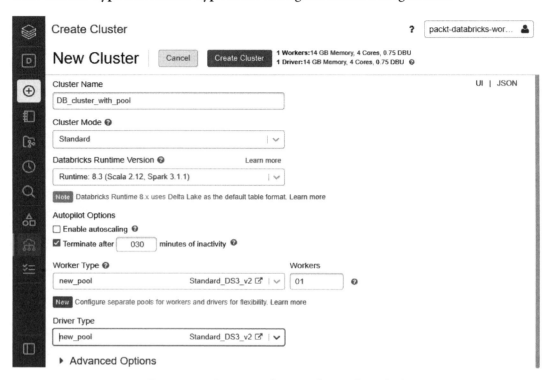

Figure 4.9 – Creating a cluster with a pool attached

Now, if we go back to the Pools in our workspace, we will spot multiple changes:

Figure 4.10 – Databricks pool after attaching a cluster

Here, we can see that the total instances has increased to three because we are using two instances from the pool – one for the driver and one for the worker in the DB_cluster_ with_pool cluster. This is what happened when we attached the cluster to the pool:

- One idle instance from new_pool was used in DB_cluster_with_pool.

- Two more instances were provisioned by the pool: one for the second node in the new_pool cluster and the other to serve as the idle instance in the pool.

Now, when we terminate the cluster, both node instances from the cluster are returned to the pool. This is confirmed by the following screenshot. Also, after 30 minutes of inactivity, two instances from the pool will be terminated and we will only have one idle instance remaining in the pool:

Figure 4.11 – Databricks pool after detaching a cluster

Now, let's walk through the best practices for Azure Databricks Pools.

Following the best practices for Azure Databricks Pools

The following list will help us learn about the best practices when using Azure Databricks pools:

- If the worker nodes and driver nodes have different node type requirements, then separate Pools must be set up.

- Pools must be configured with on-demand instances when there are short execution times expected with strict SLAs.

- Pools must be configured with spot instances when cost savings are a priority over execution times and job reliability.

- It is advisable to set the **Min Idle** configuration to 0 to avoid paying instance provider charges to Azure for idle instances. However, this can lead to an increase in cluster startup time.

- Set **Max Capacity** only when there are strict budget constraints.

- Try to set the **Min Idle** and **Idle Instance Auto Termination** configurations in such a way that even if the minimum idle instances are set to 0, the warmed instances remain in the pool so that they can be consumed by a cluster. This will ensure effective usage and optimized costs for the workloads.

This concludes learning about Databricks pools. Next, we will dive deeper into spot instances and learn how to use them with our Spark clusters!

Using spot instances

In this section, we will go through a quick tutorial on leveraging spot instances while creating our Databricks cluster. Let's begin by making a new cluster in the Databricks workspace. Create the following configuration for the cluster:

- **Cluster Name**: DB_cluster_with_spot

- **Cluster Mode**: **Standard**

- **Databricks Runtime Version**: Runtime: 8.3 (Scala 2.12, Spark 3.1.1)

- **Autoscaling**: Disabled

- **Automatic Termination**: After 30 minutes

- **Worker Type**: Standard_DS3_v2

- **Driver Type**: Standard_DS3_v2

- **Number of workers**: 1

- **Spot instances**: Enabled

It will take a few minutes for the cluster to start. The following screenshot shows that our cluster with spot instances has been initialized:

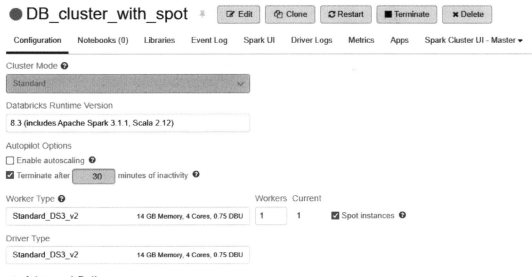

Figure 4.12 – Databricks cluster with spot instances

To confirm that we are using a cluster with spot instances, we can click on the **JSON** option to view the JSON structure of the cluster. We can find this option on the same cluster configuration page after scrolling toward the right, **UI | JSON**. In the following screenshot, SPOT_WITH_FALLBACK_AZURE signifies that our cluster has been created with spot instances:

```
1  {
2      "num_workers": 1,
3      "cluster_name": "DB_cluster_with_spot",
4      "spark_version": "8.3.x-scala2.12",
5      "spark_conf": {},
6      "azure_attributes": {
7          "first_on_demand": 1,
8          "availability": "SPOT_WITH_FALLBACK_AZURE",
9          "spot_bid_max_price": -1
10     },
11     "node_type_id": "Standard_DS3_v2",
12     "driver_node_type_id": "Standard_DS3_v2",
13     "ssh_public_keys": [],
14     "custom_tags": {},
15     "spark_env_vars": {
16         "PYSPARK_PYTHON": "/databricks/python3/bin/python3"
17     },
18     "autotermination_minutes": 30,
19     "enable_elastic_disk": true,
20     "cluster_source": "UI",
21     "init_scripts": [],
22     "cluster_id": "0728-082246-dance56"
23 }
```

Figure 4.13 – Databricks cluster with spot instances

We can also set a bidding price for using spot instances. This functionality is only possible by using the Databricks CLI, which is beyond the scope of this chapter. Next, we will look at the essential components of the Spark UI.

Following the Spark UI

The Spark UI is a web-based user interface that's used to monitor Spark jobs and is very helpful for optimizing workloads. In this section, we will learn about the major components of the Spark UI. To begin with, let's create a new Databricks cluster with the following configuration:

- **Cluster Mode**: **Standard**
- **Databricks Runtime Version**: 8.3 (includes Apache Spark 3.1.1, Scala 2.12)
- **Autoscaling**: Disabled
- **Automatic Termination**: After 30 minutes of inactivity
- **Worker Type**: Standard_DS3_v2
- **Number of workers**: 1
- **Spot instances**: Disabled
- **Driver Type**: Standard_DS3_v2

Once the cluster has started, create a new **Databricks Python notebook**. Next, let's run the following code block in a new cell:

```python
from pyspark.sql.functions import *
# Define the schema for reading streaming
schema = "time STRING, action STRING"
# Creating a streaming dataframe
stream_read = (spark
                .read
                .format("json")
                .schema(schema)
                .load("dbfs:/databricks-datasets/structured-
streaming/events/")
)
# Display the first 10 records
display(stream_read.limit(10))
```

The preceding code block creates a Spark DataFrame from JSON files and displays the first 10 records. Here, we can see that only one Spark job ran with a single stage and the stage only comprised a single task. The following screenshot confirms this:

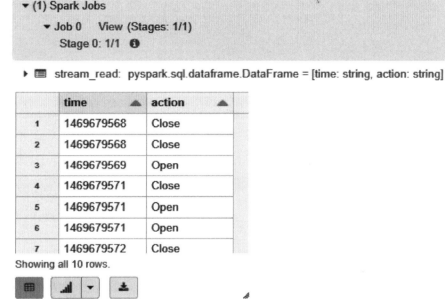

Figure 4.14 – Resulting output of the code block

Now, let's head over to the Spark UI to understand what is happing under the hood. To open the Spark UI, do the following:

1. Click on **Compute**.
2. Click on the cluster.
3. Click on **Spark UI**.

We can see the Spark UI in the following screenshot. There are various components in the Spark UI; that is, **Jobs, Stages, Storage, Environment, Executors, SQL, JDBC/ODBC Server**, and **Structured Streaming**:

Figure 4.15 – The Spark UI

Let's break down the different sections one by one.

Understanding the Jobs section

This section provides information about the different Spark jobs running on the cluster. Here, we can see two important components:

- **Event Timeline**: This tells us when the driver and executor start and stop. It is helpful to understand behaviors on auto-scaling clusters. The gaps between jobs can help indicate problems on the driver side, such as a long file scan time.

- **Completed jobs**: This table provides information about all the jobs that were completed, with the most recent job at the top. It consists of the following columns:

    I.   **Job Id** (**Job Group**): The unique identifier for a Spark job.

    II. **Description**: This consists of a link that takes us to the job-specific details.

    III. **Submitted**: The timestamp when the job was submitted to the cluster.

    IV. **Duration**: The time taken for the job to complete.

    V.   **Stages: Succeeded/Total**: The successful and total number of stages.

    VI. **Tasks**: (**for all stages**): **Succeeded/Total**: The successful and total tasks for all the stages combined.

Now, let's click on the link in the **Description** column to check the job-specific details. Here, we can several components, including **Associated SQL Query**, **Event Timeline**, **DAG Visualization**, and **Completed Stages**:

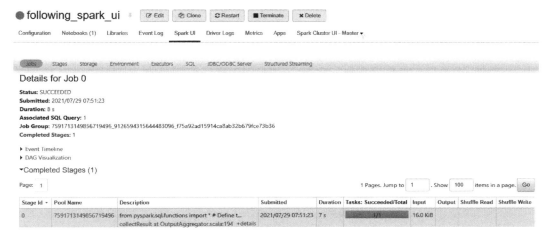

Figure 4.16 – Job-specific page in the Spark UI

Let's discuss them one by one:

- **Associated SQL Query**: This consists of a link that takes us to the SQL query diagram for the job. Most of the time, it is more helpful than a **Direct Acyclic Graph** (**DAG**) visualization. Here, we can find valuable metrics on the amount of data that was read and the number of rows returned, as shown in the following screenshot:

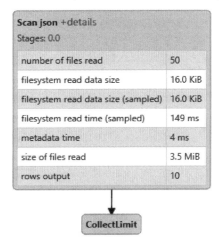

Figure 4.17– Associated SQL Query diagram

- **Event Timeline**: This visualizes when the stages started and ended.
- **DAG Visualization**: This contains a graph showing the different stages of the job.
- **Completed Stages**: Lists details about all the stages that were part of the job.

Next, we will learn about the Stages section of the Spark UI.

Understanding the Stages section

This section provides details about all the stages that were part of different jobs in the cluster.

Understanding the Storage section

This section provides details about all the DataFrames or tables that are cached in memory. We will come back to this section when we learn about Spark optimizations and caching in detail later in this book.

Understanding the Environment section

This provides information about the *Java versions* and *Spark configurations* attached to the cluster. All the Spark properties and their default or custom values, which have been set on the cluster, can be found here.

Understanding the Executors section

This provides details about the driver and worker nodes of the cluster. Things of interest here include **Cores**, **Active Tasks**, **Failed Tasks**, and **Complete Tasks**:

Summary

	RDD Blocks	Storage Memory	Disk Used	Cores	Active Tasks	Failed Tasks	Complete Tasks	Total Tasks
Active(2)	0	45 KiB / 7 GiB	0.0 B	4	0	0	1	1
Dead(0)	0	0.0 B / 0.0 B	0.0 B	0	0	0	0	0
Total(2)	0	45 KiB / 7 GiB	0.0 B	4	0	0	1	1

Figure 4.18 – The Executors summary in the Spark UI

Next, we will learn about the SQL section of the Spark UI.

Understanding the SQL section

This shows us all the completed queries in the cluster. This section also provides a SQL query diagram to help us understand the workflow of a Spark job.

Understanding the JDBC/ODBC Server section

This provides information about jobs where **Java Database Connectivity** (**JDBC**) or **Open Database Connectivity** (**ODBC**) connections have been established. These connections are usually established while working with databases such as Azure SQL Database or Azure Database for PostgreSQL.

Understanding the Structured Streaming section

This provides information about **Spark structured streaming jobs**. For example, when we are executing structured streaming jobs to process real-time data from **Azure Event Hubs** or **Apache Kafka**, this section provides us with informative metrics. It lists all the streaming jobs, the start time of each job, and other metrics such as duration and the latest batch processed.

Summary

In this chapter, we learned about designing Spark clusters for different types of workloads. We also learned about Databricks Pools, spot instances, and the Spark UI. These features help reduce costs and help make Spark jobs more efficient when they're used for the right kind of workload. Now, you will be more confident in deciding on the correct cluster configuration for a certain type of workload. Moreover, the decision you make will be influenced by useful features such as spot instances, pools, and the Spark UI.

In the next chapter, we will dive into the Databricks optimization techniques concerning Spark DataFrames. We will learn about the various techniques and their applications in various scenarios.

5

Big Data Analytics

Optimizations in **Apache Spark** play a crucial role while building big data solutions. Knowledge and experience in tuning Spark-based workloads help organizations save costs and time while running these workloads on the cloud. In this chapter, we will learn about various optimization techniques concerning **Spark DataFrames** and **big data analytics** in general. We will learn about the limitations of the `collect()` method and `inferSchema` when reading data. This will be followed by an overview of the best practices for working with **CSV** files, **Parquet** files, **Pandas** projects, and **Koalas** projects. Also, we will learn about some powerful optimization techniques, such as **column predicate pushdown**, **column pruning**, and **partitioning strategies**.

The topics covered in this chapter are as follows:

- Understanding the `collect()` method
- Understanding the use of `inferSchema`
- Learning to differentiate between CSV and Parquet
- Learning to differentiate between pandas and Koalas
- Understanding built-in Spark functions
- Learning column predicate pushdown
- Learning partitioning strategies in Spark
- Understanding Spark SQL optimizations
- Understanding bucketing in Spark

Technical requirements

To follow the hands-on tutorials in this chapter, you will need access to the following:

- A **Microsoft Azure** subscription
- **Azure Databricks**
- Azure Databricks notebooks and a Spark cluster
- Access to this book's **GitHub** repository: `https://github.com/ PacktPublishing/Optimizing-Databricks-Workload/tree/main/ Chapter05`

To start off, let's spin up a Spark cluster with the following configurations:

- **Cluster Mode**: `Standard`
- **Databricks Runtime Version**: `8.3 (includes Apache Spark 3.1.1, Scala 2.12)`
- **Autoscaling**: `Disabled`
- **Automatic Termination**: After `30` minutes of inactivity
- **Worker Type**: `Standard_DS3_v2`
- **Number of workers**: `1`
- **Spot instances**: `Disabled`
- **Driver Type**: `Standard_DS3_v2`

Now, create a new notebook and attach it to the newly created cluster to get started!

Understanding the collect() method

Spark's `collect()` function is an action, and it is used to retrieve all the elements of the **Resilient Distributed Dataset** (**RDD**) or DataFrame. We will first take a look at an example of using the function. Run the following code block:

```
from pyspark.sql.functions import *
airlines_1987_to_2008 = (
  spark
  .read
  .option("header",True)
  .option("delimiter",",")
```

```
    .option("inferSchema",True)
    .csv("dbfs:/databricks-datasets/asa/airlines/*")
)
display(airlines_1987_to_2008)
```

The preceding code block creates a Spark DataFrame and displays the first 1,000 records. Now, let's run some code with the collect() function:

```
airlines_1987_to_2008.select('Year').distinct().collect()
```

The preceding line of code returns a list of **row objects** for the Year column values. A *row object* is a collection of fields that can be iterated or accessed with an index. However, the major drawback with the function is that it brings all the data from the worker nodes to the driver. This could be very dangerous! This is because the driver can run out of memory and can potentially fail the cluster. This is why the **Out of Memory (OOM)** error is very common when using the collect() function.

In order to use the function, it is advisable to filter or aggregate the DataFrame first, before the collect() action. To demonstrate the limitations of using the function, we will run the following line of code. This simply brings the entire DataFrame onto the driver. But with the current cluster configuration, the Spark job is bound to fail:

```
airlines_1987_to_2008.collect()
```

As expected, the job fails, giving the following error:

```
org.apache.spark.SparkException: Job aborted due to stage
failure: Total size of serialized results of 53 tasks (4.0 GiB)
is bigger than spark.driver.maxResultSize 4.0 GiB.
```

The error is basically trying to tell us that the job failed because the driver does not have enough memory. Therefore, it is best to restrict the use of this function. In cases where it is being used, we should ensure that we are filtering out the data before performing the action. To print the contents of the DataFrame, we can use the display function.

Understanding the use of inferSchema

The inferSchema option is very often used to make Spark infer the data types automatically. While this approach works well for smaller datasets, performance bottlenecks can develop as the size of the data being scanned increases. In order to better understand the challenges that come with using this option for big data, we will perform a couple of experiments.

Experiment 1

In this experiment, we will re-run the code block that we ran in the previous section:

```
airlines_1987_to_2008 = (
  spark
  .read
  .option("header",True)
  .option("delimiter",",")
  .option("inferSchema",True)
  .csv("dbfs:/databricks-datasets/asa/airlines/*")
)
display(airlines_1987_to_2008)
```

The code block simply reads CSV files and creates a Spark DataFrame by automatically inferring the schema. Note the time it takes for the job to run. For us, it took *2.85 minutes*. It can take a few minutes for the preceding code block to run.

Experiment 2

Now, we will manually define the schema instead of making Spark infer it automatically. For that, we execute the following code block:

```
from pyspark.sql.types import *
manual_schema = StructType([
  StructField('Year',IntegerType(),True),
  StructField('Month',IntegerType(),True),
  StructField('DayofMonth',IntegerType(),True),
  StructField('DayOfWeek',IntegerType(),True),
  StructField('DepTime',StringType(),True),
```

We will let you take the remaining code block from the GitHub repository:

```
https://github.com/PacktPublishing/Optimizing-Databricks-Workload
```

The preceding code block defines the schema of the DataFrame that we are trying to create.

Next, it's time to create the DataFrame, and display it by passing in the schema:

```
airlines_1987_to_2008 = (
  spark
  .read
  .option("header",True)
  .option("delimiter",",")
  .schema(manual_schema)
  .csv("dbfs:/databricks-datasets/asa/airlines/*")
)
display(airlines_1987_to_2008)
```

Much to our surprise, this code block returning the same DataFrame ran much faster! For us, it only took *5.06 seconds*. But how did this happen? Let's find out.

It all comes down to our use of `inferSchema`. When using this option, Spark scans the dataset to automatically determine the correct data types. But as the data size increases, so does the size of data that Spark needs to scan. For instance, just imagine working with terabytes of data! In that case, a huge amount of time would be spent scanning the data for inferring the correct data types. In order to avoid this, we tend to manually define the schema to save time and resources.

Learning to differentiate CSV and Parquet

Data scientists are more used to CSV files than Parquet files in the majority of the cases. When they are starting to use Databricks and Spark, it becomes quite obvious that they'll continue working with CSV files. Making that switch to Parquet might be daunting at first, but in the long run, it reaps huge returns!

Let's first discuss the advantages and disadvantages of CSV and Parquet files:

Advantages of CSV files:

- CSV is the most common file type among data scientists and users.
- They are human-readable, as data is not encoded before storing. They are also easy to edit.
- Parsing CSV files is very easy, and they can be read by almost any text editor.

Advantages of Parquet files:

- Parquet files are compressed using various compression algorithms, which is why they consume less space.

- Being a columnar storage type, Parquet files are very efficient when reading and querying data.

- The file carries the schema with itself and is partitioned in nature.

- With Parquet files, Spark scans much less data than with CSV files. This leads to a reduction in costs.

Disadvantages of CSV files:

- They cannot be partitioned, and being a row-based storage type, they are not very efficient for reading and querying data.

- In the majority of use cases, when using CSV with Spark, the entire dataset needs to be scanned for working with the data.

Disadvantages of Parquet files:

- Parquet files are not human-readable.

Parquet file formats have greatly reduced storage and data scanning requirements. Also, they work very well in partitions and help to leverage Spark's parallelism. A 1 TB CSV file, when converted to Parquet, can bring down the storage requirements to as low as 100 GB in cloud storage. This helps Spark to scan less data and speed up jobs in Databricks.

Learning to differentiate Pandas and Koalas

The *Pandas* project is a very popular data transformation library in **Python** that is widely used for data analytics and data science purposes. Put simply, it's the bread and butter of data science for the majority of data scientists. But there are some limitations with the Pandas project. It is not really built for working with big data and distributed datasets. Pandas code, when executed in Databricks, only runs on the driver. This creates a performance bottleneck when the data size increases.

On the other hand, when data analysts and data scientists start working with Spark, they need to be using **PySpark** as an alternative. Due to this challenge, the creators of Databricks came up with another project and named it *Koalas*. This project has been built to allow data scientists working with Pandas to become productive with Apache Spark. It is nothing but a Pandas DataFrame API built on top of Apache Spark. Therefore, it leverages very well the parallelism offered by Spark. When switching from Pandas to Koalas, the learning curve is not steep. In fact, there is a single code base that works for both of these projects.

We will now go through a quick demonstration to learn about the differences:

1. To begin with, let's create a Spark DataFrame. Run the following code block:

```
from pyspark.sql.functions import *
airlines_1987_to_2008 = (
  spark
  .read
  .option("header",True)
  .option("delimiter",",")
  .option("inferSchema",True)
  .csv("dbfs:/databricks-datasets/asa/airlines/*")
)
display(airlines_1987_to_2008)
```

2. Next, we will try to create a Pandas DataFrame and a Koalas DataFrame using this Spark DataFrame. Note that we are working with approximately 123 million records! Run the following code to create a Pandas DataFrame:

```
pandas_df = airlines_1987_to_2008.toPandas()
```

3. As we expected, the job failed to say that the driver does not have enough memory. As we learned earlier, Spark had to bring all that data to the driver to process while using Pandas. As a result, it simply ran out of RAM. Next, let's try to create a Koalas DataFrame:

```
import databricks.koalas as ks
koalas_df = airlines_1987_to_2008.to_koalas()
```

4. This does not trigger any Spark jobs as it can be treated like a Spark transformation. Jobs are triggered when we run operations on top of the Koalas DataFrame. Now, we will do exactly that. To check the first five records, run the following code:

```
koalas_df.head()
```

5. We will now use the `describe()` function on the Koalas DataFrame, just like we use it with the Pandas DataFrame. Run the following code:

```
koalas_df.describe()
```

6. Last but not least, we will perform an aggregation to check the number of not null values in every column by `Year`. Run the following code:

```
koalas_df.groupby('Year').count()
```

As we learned, the Koalas API is the perfect fit for data scientists and analysts moving to Spark with a strong Pandas background. However, it is advisable that if a person is learning about Spark from the ground up and with no Pandas experience, then it is better to learn PySpark or another native Spark API. Next, we will learn about the differences between Spark built-in functions (higher-order functions) and **user-defined functions (UDFs)**.

Understanding built-in Spark functions

Spark gives us several built-in functions for working with DataFrames. These functions are built in such a way that they can be optimized by the catalyst optimizer. The *catalyst optimizer* is an essential component of the Spark program that helps to optimize our code using advanced programming constructs. It works very well with Spark DataFrames and built-in functions (higher-order functions). However, in the case of a UDF, the catalyst optimizer treats it as a black box. As a result, we see performance bottlenecks.

To learn about all the built-in functions in PySpark, check out the official documentation:

https://spark.apache.org/docs/latest/api/python/_modules/pyspark/sql/functions.html

In the following example, we are going to see performance differences between Spark higher-order functions and UDFs:

1. Let's begin by creating a Spark DataFrame in a new cell:

```
from pyspark.sql.types import *
manual_schema = StructType([
   StructField('Year',IntegerType(),True),
   StructField('Month',IntegerType(),True),
   StructField('DayofMonth',IntegerType(),True),
   StructField('DayOfWeek',IntegerType(),True),
   StructField('DepTime',StringType(),True),
```

We will let you take the remaining code block from the GitHub repository:

`https://github.com/PacktPublishing/Optimizing-Databricks-Workload`

The preceding code block defines the schema of the DataFrame that we are trying to create.

2. Next, it's time to create the DataFrame and display it by passing in the schema:

```
airlines_1987_to_2008 = (
  Spark
  .read
  .option("header",True)
  .option("delimiter",",")
  .schema(manual_schema)
  .csv("dbfs:/databricks-datasets/asa/airlines/*")
)
display(airlines_1987_to_2008)
```

3. In order to capture the performance differences, we will first use the `regexp_replace` higher-order function to replace the airport codes in the `Origin` column with their full names. For example, the `ATL` airport code needs to be replaced with `Hartsfield-Jackson International Airport`. With this, we will create a Spark DataFrame and then write it to **DBFS** in `delta` format:

```
built_in_df = (airlines_1987_to_2008
          .withColumn('Origin',
                    when(col('Origin') == 'ATL',regexp_
replace(col('Origin'),'ATL','Hartsfield-Jackson
International Airport'))
                    .when(col('Origin') == 'DFW',regexp_
replace(col('Origin'),'DFW','Dallas/Fort Worth
International Airport'))
                    .when(col('Origin') == 'DEN',regexp_
replace(col('Origin'),'DEN','Denver International
Airport'))
                    .when(col('Origin') == 'ORD',regexp_
replace(col('Origin'),'ORD','O Hare International
Airport'))
                    .when(col('Origin') == 'LAX',regexp_
replace(col('Origin'),'LAX','Los Angeles International
Airport'))
```

We will let you take the remaining code block from the GitHub repository: https://github.com/PacktPublishing/Optimizing-Databricks-Workload.

4. Let's note the time taken for the command to run. For us, it took 7.71 minutes. We will now perform the same operation, but this time with a UDF. To begin with, let's write the UDF:

```python
import re
airports = {'ATL':'Hartsfield-Jackson International
Airport','DFW':'Dallas/Fort Worth International
Airport','DEN':'Denver International Airport','ORD':'O
Hare International Airport','LAX':'Los Angeles
International Airport','CLT':'Hartsfield-
Jackson International Airport','LAS':'McCarran
International Airport','PHX':'Phoenix Sky
Harbor International Airport','MCO':'Orlando
International Airport','SEA':'Seattle-Tacoma
International Airport','MIA':'Miami International
Airport','IAH':'George Bush Intercontinental
Airport','JFK':'John F. Kennedy International Airport'}
def replace_origin(origin):

    for key in airports:

        if origin == key:
            replaced = re.sub(key,airports[key],origin)
            return replaced


    return None
replace_origin_udf = udf(replace_origin,StringType())
```

The preceding code block defines a UDF, replace_origin_udf, which we will use with our DataFrame to replace the same airport IATA codes with their full names.

5. Next, we will create a Spark DataFrame and write it to DBFS in the delta format:

```python
udf_df = (airlines_1987_to_2008
        .withColumn('Origin',replace_origin_
udf('Origin'))
```

```
        )
    udf_df.write.format('delta').mode('overwrite').
    save('dbfs:/udf_df')
```

This command took *9.16 minutes* for us, and it is always going to be higher than what we will get using Spark's built-in functions. The reason for this behavior is the serialization of code. When we write any Spark code, it has to be serialized, sent to the executors, and then deserialized before any output can be obtained.

In the case of Python, or more appropriately, PySpark, there is an even harder hit in performance because the code always needs to be pickled, and Spark must set up an instance of a Python interpreter on every executor. Besides the cost of serialization and deserialization, there is another issue – the catalysts optimizer doesn't understand UDFs, and therefore cannot connect any code before or after it. This is why the cost of such operations is always higher. And as the data size increases, so will the code execution times, provided the cluster configurations remain consistent.

The best practice is to use Spark built-in functions as much as possible. In the case of scenarios where these functions are not fulfilling their purpose, UDFs may be employed. This usually happens when certain complex business logic needs to be implemented. In the next section, we will learn about column predicate pushdown.

Learning column predicate pushdown

Column predicate pushdown is an optimization technique where we filter down to the level of the data source to reduce the amount of data getting scanned. This greatly enhances jobs, as Spark only reads the data that is needed for operations. For example, if we are reading from a **Postgres** database, we can push down a filter to the database to ensure that Spark only reads the required data. The same can be applied to Parquet and delta files as well. While writing Parquet and delta files to the storage account, we can partition them by one or more columns. And while reading, we can push down a filter to read only the required partitions.

In the following steps, we will look at an example of column predicate pushdown with Parquet files:

1. To get started, we will re-create our airlines DataFrame in a new cell:

```
from pyspark.sql.types import *
manual_schema = StructType([
    StructField('Year',IntegerType(),True),
    StructField('Month',IntegerType(),True),
```

```
StructField('DayofMonth',IntegerType(),True),
StructField('DayOfWeek',IntegerType(),True),
StructField('DepTime',StringType(),True),
```

We will let you take the remaining code block from the GitHub repository:

https://github.com/PacktPublishing/Optimizing-Databricks-Workload

The preceding code block defines the schema of the DataFrame that we are trying to create.

2. Next, it's time to create the DataFrame and display it by passing in the schema:

```
airlines_1987_to_2008 = (
  spark
  .read
  .option("header",True)
  .option("delimiter",",")
  .schema(manual_schema)
  .csv("dbfs:/databricks-datasets/asa/airlines/*")
)
display(airlines_1987_to_2008)
```

3. Next, we will write the DataFrame to Parquet in two ways:

    I. **Without partitioning**: Here, we will simply write the DataFrame to DBFS in the Parquet format without creating any partitions. Run the following code:

    ```
    airlines_1987_to_2008.write.format('parquet').
    mode('overwrite').save('dbfs:/columns_predicate_
    pushdown')
    ```

    II. **With partitioning**: Here, we will write the DataFrame to DBFS in Parquet by partitioning by the DayOfWeek column. Later, we will be filtering our query on this column. Run the following code:

    ```
    airlines_1987_to_2008.write.format('parquet').
    mode('overwrite').partitionBy('DayOfWeek').save('dbfs:/
    columns_predicate_pushdown_partitioned')
    ```

Now, we will run queries on the two Parquet files that we have created.

3. First, we will be filtering the Parquet file with no partitions to return the count of rows that meet the condition where `DayOfWeek` equals 7. Run the following code block:

```
without_cpp_df = (spark
                .read
                .format('parquet')
                .load('dbfs:/columns_predicate_pushdown')
                .filter(col('DayOfWeek') == 7)
)
without_cpp_df.count()
```

Note the time taken for the code to run. For us, it took *8.35 seconds*. Let's take a look at the Spark UI to better understand what is happening under the hood. Click on **Spark Jobs** under this command and select **View** next to the second job. This opens up the job page in Spark UI.

4. Click on **Associated SQL Query** to open up the query plan. Here, we can find the Parquet scan details, which tell us the amount of data scanned by Spark. The **number of files read** field indicates the total number of Parquet partition files read. The **rows output** field tells us the number of rows returned by Spark. Here, the number of rows returned equals the total number of rows in the Parquet file. If we scroll down, we can find the **Filter** box. On expanding this box, it tells us that out of 123 million records in the Parquet file, only 17 million are returned after the filtering process:

Scan parquet +details
Stages: 29.0

number of files read	93
filesystem read data size total (min, med, max)	23.7 MiB (783.2 KiB, 2.5 MiB, 4.3 MiB)
scan time total (min, med, max)	24.3 s (596 ms, 2.6 s, 4.9 s)
estimated repeated reads high size total (min, med, max)	23.7 MiB (783.2 KiB, 2.5 MiB, 4.3 MiB)
filesystem read data size (sampled) total (min, med, max)	13.6 MiB (480.5 KiB, 1292.0 KiB, 3.6 MiB)
filesystem read time (sampled) total (min, med, max)	21.5 s (530 ms, 2.3 s, 4.3 s)
metadata time	0 ms
size of files read	1464.5 MiB
estimated repeated reads low size total (min, med, max)	23.7 MiB (783.2 KiB, 2.5 MiB, 4.3 MiB)
rows output	123,534,969

Figure 5.1 – Data scanned on a non-partitioned Parquet file

5. Similarly, we will now run our code to filter on the Parquet file with partitions:

```
with_cpp_df = (spark
                .read
                .format('parquet')
                .load('dbfs:/columns_predicate_pushdown_
    partitioned')
                .filter(col('DayOfWeek') == 7)
)
with_cpp_df.count()
```

This command took only *3.73 seconds*! And it is not hard to guess why we observed this behavior. Let's take a look at the SQL query plan in the Spark UI:

Scan parquet +details
Stages: 34.0

number of files read	93
filesystem read data size total (min, med, max)	452.4 KiB (77.3 KiB, 92.6 KiB, 102.6 KiB)
scan time total (min, med, max)	6.4 s (1.0 s, 1.3 s, 1.5 s)
estimated repeated reads high size total (min, med, max)	0.0 B (0.0 B, 0.0 B, 0.0 B)
filesystem read data size (sampled) total (min, med, max)	451.7 KiB (77.2 KiB, 92.4 KiB, 102.4 KiB)
filesystem read time (sampled) total (min, med, max)	3.9 s (660 ms, 723 ms, 1.0 s)
metadata time	9 ms
size of files read	270.3 MiB
estimated repeated reads low size total (min, med, max)	0.0 B (0.0 B, 0.0 B, 0.0 B)
number of partitions read	1
rows output	17,143,178

Figure 5.2 – Data scanned on a partitioned parquet file

The query plan clearly tells us that Spark only read 17 million records. This happened because we partitioned our data by the DayOfWeek column. So, Spark had to read the partition where the filter condition met successfully. We can also verify this by taking a look at the contents inside the Parquet file directory. Run the following command in a new cell:

```
%fs ls dbfs:/columns_predicate_pushdown_partitioned
```

In the following image, we can see that the Parquet file directory is partitioned by the `DayOfWeek` column:

	path	name	size
1	dbfs:/columns_predicate_pushdown_partitioned/DayOfWeek=1/	DayOfWeek=1/	0
2	dbfs:/columns_predicate_pushdown_partitioned/DayOfWeek=2/	DayOfWeek=2/	0
3	dbfs:/columns_predicate_pushdown_partitioned/DayOfWeek=3/	DayOfWeek=3/	0
4	dbfs:/columns_predicate_pushdown_partitioned/DayOfWeek=4/	DayOfWeek=4/	0
5	dbfs:/columns_predicate_pushdown_partitioned/DayOfWeek=5/	DayOfWeek=5/	0
6	dbfs:/columns_predicate_pushdown_partitioned/DayOfWeek=6/	DayOfWeek=6/	0
7	dbfs:/columns_predicate_pushdown_partitioned/DayOfWeek=7/	DayOfWeek=7/	0
8	dbfs:/columns_predicate_pushdown_partitioned/_SUCCESS	_SUCCESS	0

Figure 5.3 – Parquet file partitioned by column

Even if we are using predicate pushdown with delta, the semantics remain the same, and we get similar performance gains. Similar to this concept, there is another optimization technique called *column pruning*. This simply means reading a subset of columns from a data store or DataFrame. For instance, say for every row we have 1,000 columns, but we only require five columns for our current purpose. In this case, we will only read five columns.

We have started learning about partitioning, and we will learn about some more partitioning strategies in the next section.

Learning partitioning strategies in Spark

In this section, we will discuss some of the useful strategies for Spark partitions and **Apache Hive** partitions. Whenever Spark processes data in memory, it breaks that data down into partitions, and these partitions are processed in the cores of the executors. These are the Spark partitions. On the other hand, Hive partitions help to organize persisted tables into parts based on columns.

Understanding Spark partitions

Before we learn about the strategies to manage Spark partitions, we need to know the number of partitions for any given DataFrame:

1. To check the Spark partitions of a given DataFrame, we use the following syntax: `dataframe.rdd.getNumPartitions()`. Also, remember that the total number of tasks doing work on a Spark DataFrame is equal to the total number of partitions of that DataFrame.

2. Next, we will learn how to check the number of records in each Spark partition. We will begin with re-creating the airlines DataFrame, but this time with **Scala**. We are shifting to Scala so that we can use the `mapPartitionsWithIndex` function. Run the following code block to create the DataFrame and display it:

```scala
%scala
// Read csv files to create Spark dataframe
val airlines_1987_to_2008 = (
  spark
  .read
  .option("header",true)
  .option("delimiter",",")
  .option("inferSchema",true)
  .csv("dbfs:/databricks-datasets/asa/airlines/*")
)
// View the dataframe
display(airlines_1987_to_2008)
```

3. Next, we will check the number of partitions in the DataFrame using the following code: `airlines_1987_to_2008.rdd.getNumPartitions`. Our DataFrame has 93 partitions! Now we will execute Scala code that displays the number of records in each partition:

```scala
%scala
display(airlines_1987_to_2008
  .rdd
  .mapPartitionsWithIndex{case (i,rows) =>
Iterator((i,rows.size))}
  .toDF("partition_number","number_of_records")
  )
```

Here, we get a DataFrame consisting of two columns:

I. `partition_number`: This gives a unique ID to every partition of the DataFrame, starting from `0`.

II. `number_of_records`: This indicates the number of records in a particular partition.

We can even create a histogram from this DataFrame to understand data skew in the DataFrame. *Data skewing* simply refers to the phenomenon where some partitions of the DataFrame are heavily loaded with records while others are not. In other words, DataFrames that have data evenly spread across partitions are not skewed in nature. In our DataFrame, roughly 87% of the partitions consist of 1.3 million to 1.5 million records.

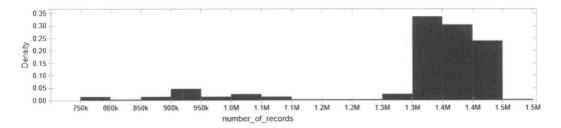

Figure 5.4 – A histogram to understand data skew

We can also use a Spark configuration, `spark.sql.files.maxPartitionBytes`, to limit the maximum size of a Spark partition when reading from Parquet, **JSON**, or **ORC** files. By default, the limit is set to 128 MB. The syntax is as follows, where N equals the maximum size in bytes:

```
spark.conf.set("spark.sql.files.maxPartitionBytes",N)
```

Apart from this, there are also two very useful functions to manage Spark partitions. These functions are used to change the number of Spark partitions of a DataFrame:

- `repartition()`: This function is used to increase or decrease the number of Spark partitions for a DataFrame. It induces a shuffle when called and is often very helpful to remove skew from a DataFrame. The syntax is `dataframe.repartition(number)`. Here, `number` designates the new partition count of the DataFrame. The `repartition` function leads to roughly equally sized partitions.

- `coalesce()`: This function is used to decrease the number of partitions and is extremely helpful when the partition count needs to be drastically reduced. Also, note that it does not lead to shuffling. The syntax is `dataframe.coalesce(number)`. Here, `number` designates the new partition count of the DataFrame. The `coalesce` function can often lead to skew in partitions.

> **Note**
>
> In Azure Databricks, to check the number of cores in a cluster programmatically, we can use `spark.sparkContext.defaultParallelism`.

If we have more cores and fewer partitions and fewer tasks being performed, then it is better to increase the partitions of the DataFrame so that all the cores get engaged. This can be very useful with the delta file format, as even though the result of such a job might spit out small files, these could be later compacted using various techniques. We will learn about these compaction techniques in a later chapter. Next, we will learn about how to effectively manage Hive partitions.

Understanding Hive partitions

Apache Hive is a data warehouse project that provides an SQL-like interface to query data stored in databases and file systems. We have already seen an example of partitioning with parquet in an earlier section. In this section, we will look at an example of partitioning with delta. We will first create a delta file partitioned by the year and month in a nested fashion. Then, using that file, we will create an external Hive table (delta table) in Databricks. We discussed the delta file format in the first chapter:

1. To get started, we will re-create our airlines DataFrame in a new cell:

```
from pyspark.sql.types import *
manual_schema = StructType([
    StructField('Year',IntegerType(),True),
    StructField('Month',IntegerType(),True),
    StructField('DayofMonth',IntegerType(),True),
    StructField('DayOfWeek',IntegerType(),True),
    StructField('DepTime',StringType(),True),
```

We will let you take the remaining code block from the GitHub repository:

https://github.com/PacktPublishing/Optimizing-Databricks-Workload

The preceding code block defines the schema of the DataFrame that we are trying to create.

2. Next, it's time to create the DataFrame and display it by passing in the schema:

```
airlines_1987_to_2008 = (
  spark
  .read
  .option("header",True)
  .option("delimiter",",")
  .schema(manual_schema)
```

```
    .csv("dbfs:/databricks-datasets/asa/airlines/*")
)
display(airlines_1987_to_2008)
```

3. Now, we will write the DataFrame to DBFS in the delta format by partitioning it.
    Run the following code to write the DataFrame as a delta file:

```
(airlines_1987_to_2008.write
 .format('delta')
 .mode('overwrite')
 .partitionBy('Year','Month')
 .save('dbfs:/airlines_1987_to_2008_partitioned')
)
```

We can check how the delta file has been partitioned using the following commands:

```
%fs ls dbfs:/airlines_1987_to_2008_partitioned
```

The preceding command displays the Year partitions. Now, we can run the next
command to check the sub-partitions inside these partitions:

```
%fs ls dbfs:/airlines_1987_to_2008_partitioned/Year=1987/
```

Here, we can see that the delta file has been partitioned at two levels. First, by Year,
and then each directory of Year is further partitioned by Month.

	path	name	size
1	dbfs:/airlines_1987_to_2008_partitioned/Year=1987/Month=10/	Month=10/	0
2	dbfs:/airlines_1987_to_2008_partitioned/Year=1987/Month=11/	Month=11/	0
3	dbfs:/airlines_1987_to_2008_partitioned/Year=1987/Month=12/	Month=12/	0

Showing all 3 rows.

Figure 5.5 – Partitioned delta file

4. Now, we will create a delta table that will be registered in the **Hive Metastore**. Run
    the following code to create the delta table:

```
%sql
CREATE TABLE airlines
USING DELTA
LOCATION 'dbfs:/airlines_1987_to_2008_partitioned'
```

We can further validate if the delta table is partitioned as expected or not. Run the `%sql` `DESCRIBE DETAIL airlines` command, and this returns a table containing a lot of useful metadata about the delta table (Hive table). Here, the `partitionColumns` field confirms that our table has been partitioned by `Year` and `Month`.

This concludes our discussion on partitioning strategies. Next, we will learn about some helpful Spark SQL optimizations.

Understanding Spark SQL optimizations

In this section, we will learn about how to write efficient Spark SQL queries, along with tips to help optimize the existing SQL queries:

- Avoid using `NOT IN` in the SQL queries, as it is a very expensive operation.
- Filter the data before performing join operations by using the `WHERE` clause before joining the tables.
- Mention the column name when using the `SELECT` clause instead of giving a `*` to select all of them. Try to use the columns required for operations instead of selecting all of them unnecessarily.
- Avoid using `LIKE` in the `WHERE` clause, as it is another expensive operation.
- Try not to join the same set of tables multiple times. Instead, write a **common table expression** (**CTE**) using the `WITH` clause to create a subquery, and use it to join the tables wherever necessary.
- When joining the same table for different conditions, use the `CASE` statements.

In the next and final section of this chapter, we will learn about bucketing in Spark.

Understanding bucketing in Spark

Bucketing is an optimization technique that helps to prevent shuffling and sorting of data during compute-heavy operations such as joins. Based on the bucketing columns we specify, data is collected in a number of *bins*. Bucketing is similar to partitioning, but in the case of partitioning, we create directories for each partition. In bucketing, we create equal-sized buckets, and data is distributed across these buckets by a hash on the value of the bucket. Partitioning is helpful when filtering data, whereas bucketing is more helpful during joins.

It is often helpful to perform bucketing on dimension tables that contain primary keys for joining. Bucketing is also helpful when join operations are being performed between small and large tables. In this section, we will go through a quick example to understand how to implement bucketing on a Hive table:

1. We will begin by creating a Spark DataFrame in a new cell. Run the following code block:

```
from pyspark.sql.functions import *
sample_df = spark.range(start = 1, end = 100000001,
step = 1, numPartitions = 100).select(col("id").
alias("key"),rand(seed = 12).alias("value"))
display(sample_df)
```

    Here, we create a Spark DataFrame, `sample_df`, with 100 million rows and 100 Spark partitions. It has two columns: `id` and `value`. Let's validate the number of Spark partitions using `sample_df.rdd.getNumPartitions()`. Now, we will validate the count of the DataFrame. Run `sample_df.count()` to confirm the count of the DataFrame.

2. Next, we will write the DataFrame as a bucket Hive table in a Parquet format. We will create 100 buckets in the table. Run the following code block to write the DataFrame as a bucketed table:

```
(sample_df
 .write
 .format('parquet')
 .mode('overwrite')
 .bucketBy(100, "key")
 .sortBy("value")
 .saveAsTable('bucketed_table')
)
```

3. Once the code block has finished executing, we can confirm if the table has been bucketed as per the configurations we have provided. To confirm this, let's run the following code:

```
%sql DESCRIBE TABLE EXTENDED bucketed_table
```

This gives us the following output:

4	# Detailed Table Information	
5	Database	default
6	Table	bucketed_table
7	Owner	root
8	Created Time	Sun Aug 15 11:20:21 UTC 2021
9	Last Access	UNKNOWN
10	Created By	Spark 3.1.0
11	Type	MANAGED
12	Provider	parquet
13	Num Buckets	100
14	Bucket Columns	[`key`]
15	Sort Columns	[`value`]
16	Location	dbfs:/user/hive/warehouse/bucketed_table
17	Serde Library	org.apache.hadoop.hive.ql.io.parquet.serde.ParquetHiveSerDe
18	InputFormat	org.apache.hadoop.hive.ql.io.parquet.MapredParquetInputFormat
19	OutputFormat	org.apache.hadoop.hive.ql.io.parquet.MapredParquetOutputFormat

Figure 5.6 – Bucketed table details

The output confirms that our table has been *bucketed* into 100 bins, using the key column.

Summary

In this chapter, we learned about several useful techniques to optimize Spark jobs when working with Spark DataFrames. We started by learning about the collect() method and when to avoid using it, and ended with a discussion of some SQL optimization best practices and bucketing. We also learned about why Parquet files and Koalas should be adopted by data scientists using Databricks.

In the next chapter, we will learn about some of the most powerful optimization techniques with **Delta Lake**. We will develop a theoretical understanding of these optimizations, and we'll write code to understand their practical use in different scenarios.

6
Databricks Delta Lake

Delta Lake is an open source storage layer that provides functionalities to data in the data lake that only exist in data warehouses. When combined with cloud storage, **Databricks** and Delta Lake lead to the formation of a **Lakehouse**. A Lakehouse simply provides the best of both worlds – **data lakes** and **data warehouses**. In today's world, a Lakehouse provides the same set of capabilities as a traditional data warehouse and at a much lower cost. This is made possible due to cheap cloud storage such as Azure Data Lake, Spark as the processing engine, and data being stored in the Delta Lake format. In this chapter, we will learn about various Delta Lake optimizations that help us build a more performant Lakehouse.

In this chapter, we will cover the following topics:

- Working with the `OPTIMIZE` and `ZORDER` commands
- Using `AUTO OPTIMIZE`
- Learning about delta caching
- Learning about dynamic partition pruning
- Understanding bloom filter indexing

Technical requirements

To follow the hands-on tutorials in the chapter, the following is required:

- An Azure subscription

- Azure Databricks

- Azure Databricks notebooks and a Spark cluster

- Access to this book's GitHub repository at `https://github.com/PacktPublishing/Optimizing-Databricks-Workload/tree/main/Chapter06`

To start, let's spin up a Spark cluster with the following configurations:

- Cluster Name: `packt-cluster`

- Cluster Mode: `Standard`

- Databricks Runtime Version: `8.3 (includes Apache Spark 3.1.1, Scala 2.12)`

- Autoscaling: `Disabled`

- Automatic Termination: After `30` minutes of inactivity

- Worker Type: `Standard_DS3_v2`

- Number of workers: `1`

- Spot instances: Disabled

- Driver Type: Same as the worker

Now, create a new notebook and attach it to the newly created cluster to get started!

Working with the OPTIMIZE and ZORDER commands

Delta lake on Databricks lets you speed up queries by changing the layout of the data stored in the cloud storage. The algorithms that support this functionality are as follows:

- **Bin-packing**: This uses the `OPTIMIZE` command and helps coalesce small files into larger ones.

- **Z-Ordering**: This uses the `ZORDER` command and helps collocate data in the same set of files. This co-locality helps reduce the amount of data that's read by Spark while processing.

Let's learn more about these two layout algorithms with a worked-out example:

1. Run the following code block:

```
from pyspark.sql.types import *
from pyspark.sql.functions import *
manual_schema = StructType([
    StructField('Year',IntegerType(),True),
    StructField('Month',IntegerType(),True),
    StructField('DayofMonth',IntegerType(),True),
    StructField('DayOfWeek',IntegerType(),True),
    StructField('DepTime',StringType(),True),
    StructField('CRSDepTime',IntegerType(),True),
    StructField('ArrTime',StringType(),True),
    StructField('CRSArrTime',IntegerType(),True),
    StructField('UniqueCarrier',StringType(),True),
```

The preceding code block defines the schema of the DataFrame that we will be creating. We will let you take the remaining code block from this book's GitHub repository: https://github.com/PacktPublishing/Optimizing-Databricks-Workload/tree/main/Chapter06. The preceding code block defines the schema of the DataFrame that we are trying to create.

2. Next, we will create a Spark DataFrame using the airlines dataset that we worked with in the previous chapters:

```
airlines_1987_to_2008 = (
    spark
    .read
    .option("header",True)
    .option("delimiter",",")
    .schema(manual_schema)
    .csv("dbfs:/databricks-datasets/asa/airlines/*")
)
display(airlines_1987_to_2008)
```

3. Now that we have a DataFrame ready, we will write it in Delta Lake format to the **Databricks File System** (**DBFS**) using the following command:

```
airlines_1987_to_2008.write.format('delta').
mode('overwrite').save('dbfs:/delta_lake_optimizations/
airlines_1987_to_2008')
```

4. We can check the number of parquet partition files that have been created at the path using the following command:

```
%fs ls dbfs:/delta_lake_optimizations/airlines_1987_
to_2008
```

Here, we can see that Spark has created 93 parquet partition files at the target location. Let's check the distribution of the size of the **parquet files** to understand how they have been created. Click on the graph icon to display a bar chart of the distribution:

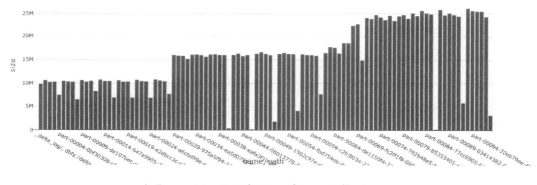

Figure 6.1 – Distribution of parquet file sizes

Here, we can see that majority of the parquet files that have been created by Spark range are between 10 MB to 25 MB in size. This means that every time Spark reads the complete **Delta file**, it has read all 93 parquet partition files. While this may not be an immediate performance bottleneck, there is some room for improvement. We will now run the OPTIMIZE and ZORDER commands to understand the performance enhancements. Run the following command to create a delta table on top of the delta file that we have written to DBFS:

```
%sql
CREATE TABLE airlines_unoptimized
```

```
USING DELTA
LOCATION 'dbfs:/delta_lake_optimizations/airlines_1987_
to_2008'
```

5. Next, we will run the OPTIMIZE and ZORDER commands. The syntax for both of them is as follows:

    I. **Bin-packing**: OPTIMIZE delta.'delta_file_path' or OPTIMIZE delta_table. Here, delta_file_path is the location of the Delta Lake file and delta_table is the name of the delta table.

    II. **Z-Ordering**: ZORDER BY (columns). Here, columns indicates the names of the columns based on which we are Z-Ordering.

6. To run the OPTIMIZE and ZORDER commands on the delta table we have created, run the following code block:

```
%sql
OPTIMIZE airlines_unoptimized
ZORDER BY (Year, Origin)
```

Note that this is a time-consuming process and that we will have to wait for a few minutes before the execution completes.

7. Here, we are compacting the airlines_unoptimized delta table and co-locating data by the Year and Origin columns:

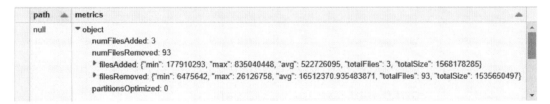

Figure 6.2 – Metrics collected after bin-packing

Once the execution completes, we can check the metrics and see that numFilesAdded and numFilesRemoved are 3 and 93, respectively. This means that 3 parquet partition files were written to the delta file directory. Also, the OPTIMIZE command leads to the creation of a new version of the delta table. numFilesRemoved does not imply that parquet files were deleted; instead, they were not carried forward to the newer version of the delta table.

8. We can check the distribution again using the following code to find that the three parquet partition files are of a much larger size – 178 MB, 555 MB, and 835 MB:

```
%fs ls dbfs:/delta_lake_optimizations/airlines_1987_
to_2008
```

By default, the Bin-Packing algorithm attempts to write the data in parquet files up to 1 GB in size.

9. We can also run the following command to check the table's version history:

```
%sql DESCRIBE HISTORY airlines_unoptimized
```

Here, we have two versions:

I.   Version 0: *Without* Bin-Packing and Z-Ordering

II. Version 1: *With* Bin-Packing and Z-Ordering

10. We will now run queries to compare the performance of both versions of the delta table. To begin with, we will run the following query on version 0. Here, we are returning the count of records in the table where the year belongs to the 1990s and the origin airport is among SYR, JFK, and LAX:

```
%sql
SELECT COUNT(*) FROM airlines_unoptimized VERSION AS OF 0
WHERE Year LIKE '19%' AND Origin IN ('SYR','JFK','LAX')
```

This query took *11.65 seconds* to execute.

11. Next, we will run the same query on version 1 where we have performed Bin-Packing and Z-Ordered on the Year and Origin columns:

```
%sql
SELECT COUNT(*) FROM airlines_unoptimized VERSION AS OF 1
WHERE Year LIKE '19%' AND Origin IN ('SYR','JFK','LAX')
```

This query took only *6.91 seconds*! This happened due to the following two reasons:

I.   We have coalesced 93 smaller files into three larger files. This prevents Spark from reading too many small files.

II. We have co-located data on the same columns that we are filtering on.

Hence, OPTIMIZE and ZORDER can be used to speed up Databricks queries. As a best practice, ZORDER should be used on columns that are commonly used in queries to filter data and have high cardinality. But *Z-Ordering* on too many columns can also degrade performance. Hence, the columns to Z-Order on should be chosen wisely. *Bin-packing* should always be used when different transactions such as inserts, deletes, or updates are being executed on a delta table. Also, it is an idempotent process, meaning that if the OPTIMIZE command is run twice on a table, the second run will have no effect.

This concludes this section on Bin-Packing and Z-Ordering. Next, we will learn about Auto Optimize.

Using Auto Optimize

Auto Optimize is a feature that helps us automatically compact small files while an individual writes to a delta table. Unlike bin-packing, we do not need to run a command every time Auto Optimize is executed. It consists of two components:

- **Optimized Writes**: Databricks dynamically optimizes Spark partition sizes to write 128 MB chunks of table partitions.

- **Auto Compaction**: Here, Databricks runs an optimized job when the data writing process has been completed and compacts small files. It tries to coalesce small files into 128 MB files. This works on data that has the greatest number of small files.

Next, we will learn about the Spark configurations for Auto Optimize and go through a worked-out example to understand how it works:

1. To enable Auto Optimize for all new tables, we need to run the following Spark configuration code:

```sql
%sql
set spark.databricks.delta.properties.defaults.
autoOptimize.optimizeWrite = true;
set spark.databricks.delta.properties.defaults.
autoOptimize.autoCompact = true;
```

2. Now, let's go through a worked-out example where we will write data in Delta Lake format and understand parquet partition file size distribution after enabling Auto Optimize. Run the following code block:

```
from pyspark.sql.types import *
from pyspark.sql.functions import *
manual_schema = StructType([
```

```
StructField('Year',IntegerType(),True),
StructField('Month',IntegerType(),True),
StructField('DayofMonth',IntegerType(),True),
StructField('DayOfWeek',IntegerType(),True),
StructField('DepTime',StringType(),True),
StructField('CRSDepTime',IntegerType(),True),
StructField('ArrTime',StringType(),True),
StructField('CRSArrTime',IntegerType(),True),
StructField('UniqueCarrier',StringType(),True),
```

We will let you take the remaining code block from this book's GitHub repository. The preceding code block defines the schema of the DataFrame that we are trying to create.

3. Next, we will create a Spark DataFrame using the airlines dataset that we worked with in the previous chapters:

```
airlines_1987_to_2008 = (
  spark
  .read
  .option("header",True)
  .option("delimiter",",")
  .schema(manual_schema)
  .csv("dbfs:/databricks-datasets/asa/airlines/*")
)
display(airlines_1987_to_2008)
```

4. Now that we have a DataFrame ready, we will write it in the Delta Lake format to DBFS using the following command:

```
airlines_1987_to_2008.write.format('delta').
mode('overwrite').save('dbfs:/delta_lake_optimizations/
airlines_1987_to_2008_auto_optimize')
```

5. Next, let's look at the distribution of the parquet file size using the following code:

```
%fs ls dbfs:/delta_lake_optimizations/airlines_1987_
to_2008_auto_optimize
```

6. Here, we can see that only 19 parquet files have been written. Click on the graph icon to display a bar chart of the distribution. We can see that the majority of the parquet file sizes are between 75 MB to 100 MB:

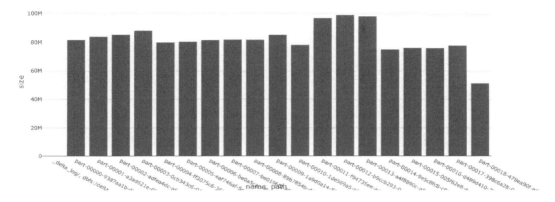

Figure 6.3 – Parquet files size distribution after performing Auto Optimize

This confirms that Auto Optimize has been applied to our newly written file in delta format. But Auto Optimize may not always be useful in every scenario. To understand this, we will learn when to opt in and when to opt out of the Auto Optimize features.

Understanding optimized writes

Optimized writes help dynamically optimize Spark partition sizes to write 128 MB chunks of table partitions. Here are some best practices regarding optimized writes:

- Optimized writes involve shuffling data across the executors, so they should only be used if a minutes' worth of latency is acceptable in streaming jobs.

- It should be used when SQL commands such as UPDATE, DELETE, and more are frequently used.

- It should not be used when terabytes of data is being processed and storage optimized node instances are not available.

Next, let's learn about Auto Compaction.

Understanding Auto Compaction

Auto Compaction tries to coalesce small files into 128 MB files and works on data that has the greatest number of small files. Here are some best practices regarding optimized writes:

- Auto Compaction should be used when a minutes' worth of latency is acceptable in streaming jobs.

- If Bin-Packing is not being done on a delta table, Auto Compaction should be used.

- This feature should not be used when operations such as DELETE, UPDATE, and more are being applied on a Delta table. This is because Auto Compaction is performed on a table after the write has succeeded. Hence, there could be a transactional conflict between the jobs.

> **Note**
> If Auto Compaction fails due to a conflict, Databricks does not fail or retry the compaction.

This concludes this section on Auto Optimize. In the next section, we will learn about delta caching.

Learning about delta caching

Delta caching is an optimization technique that helps speed up queries by storing the data in the cluster node's local storage. The delta cache stores local copies of data that resides in remote locations such as **Azure Data Lake** or **Azure Blob Storage**. It improves the performance of a wide range of queries but cannot store the results of arbitrary subqueries.

Once delta caching has been enabled, any data that is fetched from an external location is automatically added to the cache. This process does not require action. To preload data into the delta cache, the CACHE command can be used. Any changes that have been made to the data persisted in the delta cache are automatically detected by the delta cache. The easiest way to use delta caching is to provision a cluster with **Standard_L** series worker types (**Delta Cache Accelerated**).

Now, we will go through a worked-out example with delta caching. To begin with, we will provide a new cluster with the following configurations:

- Cluster Name: `delta-caching`
- Cluster Mode: `Standard`

- Databricks Runtime Version: `8.3` (includes Apache Spark `3.1.1`, Scala `2.12`)

- Autoscaling: `Disabled`

- Automatic Termination: After `30` minutes of inactivity

- Worker Type: `Standard_L8s_v2`

- Number of workers: `1`

- Spot instances: Disabled

- Driver Type: Same as the worker

Note that the **Standard_L8s_v2** worker type might not be available in all regions. Hence, it is recommended to use the **East US** region for the Azure Databricks workspace. Now, let's create a new notebook and attach it to the newly created cluster to get started:

1. Run the following code block:

```
From pyspark.sql.types import *
from pyspark.sql.functions import *
manual_schema = StructType([
    StructField('Year',IntegerType(),True),
    StructField('Month',IntegerType(),True),
    StructField('DayofMonth',IntegerType(),True),
    StructField('DayOfWeek',IntegerType(),True),
    StructField('DepTime',StringType(),True),
    StructField('CRSDepTime',IntegerType(),True),
    StructField('ArrTime',StringType(),True),
    StructField('CRSArrTime',IntegerType(),True),
    StructField('UniqueCarrier',StringType(),True),
```

We will let you take the remaining code block from this book's GitHub repository: `https://github.com/PacktPublishing/Optimizing-Databricks-Workload`. The preceding code block defines the schema of the DataFrame that we are trying to create.

2. Next, we will create a Spark DataFrame using the airlines dataset that we have worked with in the previous chapters:

```
Airlines_1987_to_2008 = (
  spark
  .read
  .option("header",True)
  .option("delimiter",",")
  .schema(manual_schema)
  .csv("dbfs:/databricks-datasets/asa/airlines/*")
)
display(airlines_1987_to_2008)
```

3. Now that we have a DataFrame ready, we will write it in Delta Lake format to DBFS using the following command:

```
airlines_1987_to_2008.write.format('delta').
mode('overwrite').save('dbfs:/delta_lake_optimizations/
airlines_1987_to_2008_delta_caching')
```

4. Next, we will create a delta table. Run the following code block:

```
%sql
CREATE TABLE airlines_delta_caching
USING DELTA
LOCATION 'dbfs:/delta_lake_optimizations/airlines_1987_
to_2008_delta_caching'
```

5. To confirm if delta caching is enabled on the cluster, we can run the following command:

```
spark.conf.get("spark.databricks.io.cache.enabled")
```

The output will be true. This confirms that delta caching has been enabled on the cluster.

6. Now, we will cache the data. Run the following command to store the data in the delta cache:

```
%sql CACHE SELECT * FROM airlines_delta_caching
```

7. We can also monitor the cache from the Spark UI. Head over to the cluster's Spark UI and click on **Storage**. Here, the **Data Written to IO Cache** field gives the total size of the data that's been written to the delta cache:

Storage

Parquet IO Cache

Host	Disk Usage	Max Disk Usage Limit	Percent Disk Usage	Metadata Cache Size	Max Metadata Cache Size Limit	Percent Metadata Usage
10.139.64.6	1464.0 MiB	960.0 GiB	0 %	473.0 KiB	19.2 GiB	0 %
Total	1464.0 MiB	960.0 GiB	0 %	473.0 KiB	19.2 GiB	0 %

Data Read from External Filesystem	Data Read from IO Cache	Data Written to IO Cache	Estimated Size of Repeatedly Read Data	Cache Metadata Manager Peak Disk Usage
25.3 GiB	0.0 B	3.0 GiB	0.0 B (0 %) - 0.0 B (0 %)	5.1 KiB

Figure 6.4 – Monitoring delta caching

When a worker node reaches 100% disk usage, the cache manager discards cache entries that are used the least. This is done to make way for new data. You can try running some ad hoc queries on the delta table to experience the performance gains for delta caching.

8. To disable delta caching, we can run the following command:

```
spark.conf.set("spark.databricks.io.cache.
enabled","false")
```

Disabling delta caching does not lead to dropping data from local storage. It only prevents queries from writing data to the cache or reading from it. Do not forget to terminate the **delta-caching** cluster!

With this, we have concluded this section on delta caching. Next, we will learn about **dynamic partition pruning** in Databricks.

Learning about dynamic partition pruning

Dynamic partition pruning is a *data-skipping technique* that can drastically speed up query execution time. Delta lake collects metadata on the partition files it manages so that data can be skipped without the need to access it. This technique is very useful for *star schema* types of queries as it can dynamically skip partitions and their respective files. Using this technique, we can prune the partitions of a fact table during the join to a dimension table. This is made possible when the filter that's applied to a dimension table to prune its partitions is dynamically applied to the fact table. We will now learn how this technique works by looking at an example. Before we get started, do not forget to spin up the **packt-cluster** cluster!

In this example, we will demonstrate a star schema model by joining a fact table and a dimension table. A star schema is one of the simplest ways to build a data warehouse. It consists of one or more fact tables referencing any number of dimension tables. A **fact table** stores data to be analyzed, whereas a dimension table stores data about the ways a fact table data can be analyzed.

Let's start creating our fact delta table:

1. Create a new cell and run the following code block:

```python
from pyspark.sql.types import *
from pyspark.sql.functions import *
manual_schema = StructType([
    StructField('Year',IntegerType(),True),
    StructField('Month',IntegerType(),True),
    StructField('DayofMonth',IntegerType(),True),
    StructField('DayOfWeek',IntegerType(),True),
    StructField('DepTime',StringType(),True),
    StructField('CRSDepTime',IntegerType(),True),
    StructField('ArrTime',StringType(),True),
    StructField('CRSArrTime',IntegerType(),True),
    StructField('UniqueCarrier',StringType(),True),
```

We will let you take the remaining code block from this book's GitHub repository: `https://github.com/PacktPublishing/Optimizing-Databricks-Workload`. The previous code block defines the schema of the DataFrame that we are trying to create.

2. Next, we will create a Spark DataFrame using the airlines dataset and write it to DBFS in delta format:

```python
airlines_1987_to_2008 = (
  spark
  .read
  .option("header",True)
  .option("delimiter",",")
  .schema(manual_schema)
  .csv("dbfs:/databricks-datasets/asa/airlines/*")
)
```

```
airlines_1987_to_2008.write.format('delta').
mode('overwrite').partitionBy('Origin').save('dbfs:/
dynamic_partition_pruning/fact_table')
```

3. We can check the parquet partition files that have been created using the following command:

```
%fs ls dbfs:/dynamic_partition_pruning/fact_table
```

4. Now, let's create a delta table using the data. Run the following code block:

```
%sql
CREATE TABLE airlines_fact_table
USING DELTA
LOCATION 'dbfs:/dynamic_partition_pruning/fact_table'
```

5. Now, we need to verify the number of files and the size of the fact table. To do this, we can run the code in a new cell:

```
%sql DESCRIBE DETAIL airlines_fact_table
```

This command provides some important information about the delta table, as follows:

   I.   partitionColumns: This specifies the columns based on which the delta table has been partitioned. Our delta table has been partitioned on the Origin column.

   II. numFiles: This states the number of parquet partition files in the delta table. The table consists of 22,079 files.

   III. sizeInBytes: This tells us the size of the delta table. Our delta table is about 1.7 GB in size.

6. Next, we will create the dimension table. Run the following code block to create the dimension table:

```
%sql
CREATE TABLE airlines_dim_table(
iata_code STRING NOT NULL,
airport_name STRING NOT NULL
)
```

```
USING DELTA
PARTITIONED BY (iata_code)
LOCATION 'dbfs:/dynamic_file_pruning/dim_table'
```

7.   This creates a delta table with no data. Now, let's insert some records into the table using the following code block:

```
%sql
INSERT INTO airlines_dim_table(iata_code,airport_name)
VALUES
('ABE','Lehigh Valley International Airport'),
('ABI','Abilene Regional Airport'),
('ABQ','Albuquerque International Sunport'),
('ABY','Southwest Georgia Regional Airport'),
('ACK','Nantucket Memorial Airport'),
('ACT','Waco Regional Airport'),
('ACV','Arcata Airport'),
('ACY','Atlantic City International Airport'),
('ADQ','Kodiak Airport'),
('AEX','Alexandria International Airport'),
('AGS','Augusta Regional Airport'),
('AKN','King Salmon Airport'),
('ALB','Albany International Airport'),
('ALO','Waterloo Regional Airport'),
('AMA','Rick Husband Amarillo International Airport'),
```

We will let you take the remaining code block from this book's GitHub repository. The preceding code block inserts 311 new records into the dimension table.

8.   Finally, it is time to run a query! Run the following code block:

```
%sql
SELECT AVG(CAST(f.ActualElapsedTime as DOUBLE)) as
AvgActualElapsedTime
FROM airlines_fact_table AS f
INNER JOIN airlines_dim_table AS d
ON f.Origin = d.iata_code
```

```
WHERE d.airport_name in ('San Diego International
Airport','John F. Kennedy International Airport','Los
Angeles International Airport','Hartsfield-Jackson
Atlanta International Airport')
```

This query returns the average time that's elapsed on a flight where the origin airport is among the four airports given in the WHERE clause. For us, this query took about *10.62 seconds* to finish executing. Now, let's take a look at what is happening behind the scenes.

9. Click on **Spark Jobs** and click on **View** next to the last job that ran. The Spark UI will open.

10. Click on the number next to **Associated SQL Query**.

11. Here, we can see that our dimension table is getting scanned first, followed by the fact table. But before the fact table gets scanned, something interesting happens:

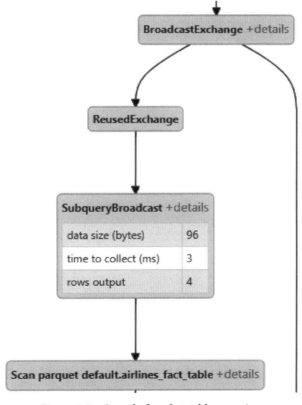

Figure 6.5 – Steps before fact table scanning

Here, four records are being filtered from the dimension table and this filter is also being applied to the fact table. We can confirm this by taking a look at the details of the fact table scan.

Here, only 372 files were read, while the fact table contains 22,079 files! The `dynamic partition pruning time` field also confirms that the technique has been applied. Furthermore, only four partitions from the fact table were read from the fact table, resulting in about 13 million records for the join.

12. Next, we will compare this performance by disabling dynamic partition pruning. To disable it, we can run the following line of code:

```
spark.conf.set('spark.databricks.optimizer.
dynamicPartitionPruning','false'
```

This Spark configuration is enabled by default.

13. Now, we will run the same query in a new cell:

```
%sql
SELECT AVG(CAST(f.ActualElapsedTime as DOUBLE)) as
AvgActualElapsedTime
FROM airlines_fact_table AS f
INNER JOIN airlines_dim_table AS d
ON f.Origin = d.iata_code
WHERE d.airport_name in ('San Diego International
Airport','John F. Kennedy International Airport','Los
Angeles International Airport','Hartsfield-Jackson
Atlanta International Airport')
```

This query took *4.44 minutes* to run! This means that with dynamic partition pruning, our query ran *96* times faster. This happened because Spark had to read the entire table before the join. We can confirm this from the Spark UI by looking at the **Associated SQL Query** diagram.

It is evident that all 22,079 files of the fact table had to be read and no data skipping was involved. With this, we can conclude this section on dynamic partition pruning. Last but not the least, we will learn about **bloom filter indexing** in Databricks.

Understanding bloom filter indexing

A **bloom filter index** is a data structure that provides data skipping on columns, especially on fields containing arbitrary text. The filter works by either stating that certain data is definitely not in a file or that it is probably in the file, which is defined by a **false positive probability** (**FPP**). The bloom filter index can help speed up *needle in a haystack* type of queries, which are not sped up by other techniques.

Let's go through a worked-out example that illustrates the performance benefits of using a bloom filter index:

1. We will start by checking the Spark configuration for bloom filter indexes. Run the following line of code in a new cell:

```
spark.conf.get('spark.databricks.io.skipping.bloomFilter.
enabled')
```

By default, it is true.

2. Now, we can start creating our very first bloom filter index! To begin with, let's create a delta table using the following block of code:

```
%sql
CREATE OR REPLACE TABLE bloom_filter_test (
   id BIGINT NOT NULL,
   hashed_col_a STRING NOT NULL,
   hashed_col_b STRING NOT NULL
)
USING DELTA
LOCATION 'dbfs:/bloom_filter_test'
```

This delta table will have three columns:

I. `id`: This is a regular primary key column.

II. `hashed_col_a`: We will use a hashing function to insert values into this column. Then, we will apply a bloom filter index to it.

III. `hashed_col_b`: We will use a hashing function to insert values into this column. However, we will not apply a bloom filter to this column. This is for performance comparison purposes.

3. Next, we will create the bloom filter index using the following block of code:

```sql
%sql
CREATE BLOOMFILTER INDEX
ON TABLE bloom_filter_test
FOR COLUMNS(hashed_col_a OPTIONS (fpp=0.1,
numItems=1000000))
```

Here, the two OPTIONS have been defined as follows:

I. fpp: This defines the false positivity rate. It influences the size of the bloom filter index and the value must be larger than 0 and smaller than 1. The lower fpp is, the more accurate it will be.

II. numItems: This defines the total number of distinct items a file can contain.

4. Next, we will insert records into our newly created delta table:

```sql
%sql
WITH cte (
  SELECT
    monotonically_increasing_id() AS id,
    sha(CAST(id AS string)) AS hashed_col_a,
    sha(CAST(id AS string)) AS hashed_col_b
  FROM
    RANGE(0, 1000000, 1, 100)
)
INSERT INTO bloom_filter_test
SELECT id, hashed_col_a, hashed_col_b
FROM cte
```

The preceding code block inserts 1 million records into the bloom_filter_test delta table.

5. We can run the query to get a glimpse of the data:

```sql
%sql SELECT * FROM bloom_filter_test
```

6. Note that the `hashed_col_a` and `hashed_col_b` columns consist of identical data. This has been purposely done so that we can get a performance comparison using the bloom filter index. Next, we will run a query and filter on the `hashed_col_a` column, which is where the bloom filter index has already been applied:

```sql
%sql
SELECT *
FROM bloom_filter_test
WHERE hashed_col_a IN ('79816ecb0a75e0b29ec93a3e4845cf4
f0b5d4d4d','3554dce55f341edd431fc711f6816673f081452d',
'cf2f328d24859d56d55d2b610b12525e60b21895')
```

This query took *4.47 seconds* to execute. We can take a look at the Spark UI as well. The **Associated SQL Query** section of the job does reflect some positives:

Scan parquet with Bloom Filters default.bloom_filter_test +details
Stages: 244.0 245.0

number of files read	100
filesystem read data size total (min, med, max)	58.0 MiB (14.3 MiB, 14.3 MiB, 15.1 MiB)
scan time total (min, med, max)	115 ms (2 ms, 2 ms, 109 ms)
estimated repeated reads high size total (min, med, max)	58.0 MiB (14.3 MiB, 14.3 MiB, 15.1 MiB)
filesystem read data size (sampled) total (min, med, max)	58.0 MiB (14.3 MiB, 14.3 MiB, 15.1 MiB)
filesystem read time (sampled) total (min, med, max)	4.5 s (980 ms, 1.2 s, 1.3 s)
metadata time	0 ms
skipping time (ms) total (min, med, max)	7.5 s (1.8 s, 1.9 s, 2.0 s)
size of files read	81.1 MiB
number of file splits skipped	99
number of file splits read	1
estimated repeated reads low size total (min, med, max)	58.0 MiB (14.3 MiB, 14.3 MiB, 15.1 MiB)
rows output	10,000

Figure 6.6 – The Spark UI of the query with a bloom filter index

From the preceding screenshot, we can see that out of the 1 million records, only 10,000 records were returned for processing.

7. Next, we will run a query by filtering on the `hashed_col_b` column, where no
    index has been applied:

```sql
%sql
SELECT *
FROM bloom_filter_test
WHERE hashed_col_b IN ('79816ecb0a75e0b29ec93a3e4845cf4f0b
5d4d4d','3554dce55f341edd431fc711f6816673f081452d',
'cf2f328d24859d56d55d2b610b12525e60b21895')
```

This query took *6.44 seconds* to execute. Thus, we can see performance gains by
using bloom filter indexing. This is also confirmed with the help of the Spark UI:

Scan parquet with Bloom Filters default.bloom_filter_test +details
Stages: 4.0 5.0

number of files read	100
filesystem read data size total (min, med, max)	81.1 MiB (20.3 MiB, 20.3 MiB, 20.3 MiB)
scan time total (min, med, max)	10.5 s (2.6 s, 2.6 s, 2.8 s)
estimated repeated reads high size total (min, med, max)	81.1 MiB (20.3 MiB, 20.3 MiB, 20.3 MiB)
filesystem read data size (sampled) total (min, med, max)	81.1 MiB (20.3 MiB, 20.3 MiB, 20.3 MiB)
filesystem read time (sampled) total (min, med, max)	6.8 s (1.6 s, 1.7 s, 1.9 s)
metadata time	2 ms
skipping time (ms) total (min, med, max)	0 ms (0 ms, 0 ms, 0 ms)
size of files read	81.1 MiB
number of file splits skipped	0
number of file splits read	0
estimated repeated reads low size total (min, med, max)	81.1 MiB (20.3 MiB, 20.3 MiB, 20.3 MiB)
rows output	1,000,000

Figure 6.7 – The Spark UI of the query without a bloom filter index

Here, we can see that all 1 million records were returned for processing. This concludes
this section on bloom filter indexing and brings us to the end of this chapter.

Summary

In this chapter, we learned about several optimization techniques concerning Databricks Delta Lake. We started with file compaction and clustering techniques and ended with techniques for efficient data skipping. These optimization techniques play a crucial role in making querying and data engineering workloads in Databricks quicker and more efficient.

In the next chapter, we will learn about another set of Spark optimization techniques related to Spark core. We will develop a theoretical understanding of these optimizations and write code to understand their practical usage in different scenarios.

7
Spark Core

Performance tuning in **Apache Spark** plays an instrumental role in running efficient big data workloads. More often than not, the optimization techniques employed to prevent the shuffling and skewing of data drastically improve performance. In this chapter, we will learn about the Spark optimization techniques directly related to **Spark Core** that help prevent the shuffling and skewing of data.

We will begin by learning about broadcast joins and how they are different from traditional joins in Spark. Next, we will learn about **Apache Arrow**, its integration with the **Python pandas** project, and how it improves the performance of Pandas code in **Azure Databricks**. We will also learn about shuffle partitions, Spark caching, and **adaptive query execution** (**AQE**). Shuffle partitions can often become performance bottlenecks, and it is important that we learn how to tune them. Spark caching is another popular optimization technique that helps to speed up queries on the same data without having to re-read it from the source. Last but not least, AQE helps to automatically optimize data engineering workloads. The topics covered in this chapter are as follows:

- Learning about broadcast joins
- Learning about Apache Arrow in Pandas
- Understanding shuffle partitions
- Understanding caching in Spark
- Learning about AQE

Technical requirements

To follow the hands-on tutorials in this chapter, the following are required:

- A **Microsoft Azure** subscription
- Azure Databricks
- Azure Databricks notebooks and a Spark cluster
- Access to this book's **GitHub** repository:

  `https://github.com/PacktPublishing/Optimizing-Databricks-`
  `Workload/tree/main/Chapter07`

To start off, let's spin up a Spark cluster with the following configurations:

- **Cluster Name**: `packt-cluster`
- **Cluster Mode: Standard**
- **Databricks Runtime Version**: `8.3` (includes Apache Spark 3.1.1, Scala 2.12)
- **Autoscaling**: Disabled
- **Automatic Termination**: After `30` minutes of inactivity
- **Worker Type**: `Standard_DS3_v2`
- **Number of workers**: 2
- **Spot instances**: Disabled
- **Driver Type**: `Standard_DS3_v2`

Now, create a new notebook and attach it to the newly created cluster to get started!

Learning about broadcast joins

In **ETL** operations, we need to perform join operations between new data and lookup tables or historical tables. In such scenarios, a join operation is performed between a large DataFrame (millions of records) and a small DataFrame (hundreds of records). A standard join between a large and small DataFrame incurs a shuffle between the worker nodes of the cluster. This happens because all the matching data needs to be shuffled to every node of the cluster. While this process is computationally expensive, it also leads to performance bottlenecks due to network overheads on account of shuffling. Here, **broadcast joins** come to the rescue! With the help of broadcast joins, Spark duplicates the smaller DataFrame on every node of the cluster, thereby avoiding the cost of shuffling the large DataFrame.

We can better understand the difference between a standard join and a broadcast join with the help of the following diagram. In the case of a standard join, the partitions of both the DataFrames need to shuffle across worker nodes or executors so that matching records based on the join condition can be joined. In the case of a broadcast join, Spark sends a copy of the smaller DataFrame to each node or executor so that it can be joined with the respective partition of the larger DataFrame.

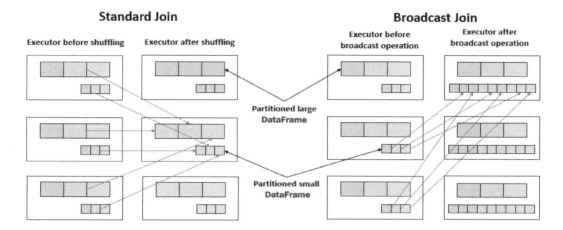

Figure 7.1 – A standard join and a broadcast join

Now, we will go through a worked-out example to better understand the performance comparisons of both of these joins:

1. First, we will create a large DataFrame using the airlines dataset in Databricks. Run the following code block to define the schema of the DataFrame:

```
from pyspark.sql.types import *
from pyspark.sql.functions import *
manual_schema = StructType([
  StructField('Year',IntegerType(),True),
  StructField('Month',IntegerType(),True),
  StructField('DayofMonth',IntegerType(),True),
  StructField('DayOfWeek',IntegerType(),True),
  StructField('DepTime',StringType(),True),
  StructField('CRSDepTime',IntegerType(),True),
  StructField('ArrTime',StringType(),True),
```

We will let you take the remaining code block from the GitHub repository:

`https://github.com/PacktPublishing/Optimizing-Databricks-Workload`

2. Next, we will create the DataFrame using the manually defined schema, using the following code block:

```
airlines_1987_to_2008 = (
  spark
  .read
  .option("header",True)
  .option("delimiter",",")
  .schema(manual_schema)
  .csv("dbfs:/databricks-datasets/asa/airlines/*")
)
```

3. We will now create a lookup Delta table and insert records in this table. Later, we will use this Delta table as our smaller DataFrame that will be joined with the airlines DataFrame. Run the following code block to create the lookup Delta table:

```
%sql
CREATE TABLE lookup_table(
iata_code STRING NOT NULL,
airport_name STRING NOT NULL
)
USING DELTA
LOCATION 'dbfs:/broadcast_joins/lookup_table'
```

4. Next, we will insert records in the Delta table using the following code block:

```
%sql
INSERT INTO lookup_table(iata_code,airport_name) VALUES
('ABE','Lehigh Valley International Airport'),
('ABI','Abilene Regional Airport'),
('ABQ','Albuquerque International Sunport'),
('ABY','Southwest Georgia Regional Airport'),
('ACK','Nantucket Memorial Airport'),
('ACT','Waco Regional Airport'),
('ACV','Arcata Airport'),
```

```
('ACY','Atlantic City International Airport'),
('ADQ','Kodiak Airport'),
```

We will let you take the remaining code block from the GitHub repository:

```
https://github.com/PacktPublishing/Optimizing-Databricks-
Workload
```

5. Now, we will perform a standard join using the following code block. Here, we will be performing an inner join between the two DataFrames and then writing the resulting DataFrame to the **Databricks File System** (**DBFS**) in the Delta file format:

```
lookup_table = spark.table("lookup_table")
standard_join = (airlines_1987_to_2008
                .join(lookup_table,airlines_1987_
to_2008.Origin == lookup_table.iata_code,"inner")
                .drop('Origin')
                )
standard_join.write.format('delta').mode('overwrite').
save('dbfs:/broadcast_joins/standard_join')
```

This code was executed in *21.60 minutes*. Next, we will perform a broadcast join to see whether we can improve performance.

6. Run the following code block to perform a broadcast join. Note the change in the following code block. We just need to use the `broadcast` function on the smaller DataFrame to mark it as small enough to be used in a broadcast join:

```
lookup_table = spark.table("lookup_table")
broadcast_join = (airlines_1987_to_2008
                .join(broadcast(lookup_
table),airlines_1987_to_2008.Origin == lookup_table.iata_
code,"inner").drop('Origin')
                )
broadcast_join.write.format('delta').mode('overwrite').
save('dbfs:/broadcast_joins/broadcast_join')
```

A broadcast join on the same DataFrames took nearly *17.34 minutes*. Therefore, it is quite evident that broadcast joins can help to optimize join operations when one of the DataFrames is small enough to be sent to every node of the cluster.

The catch here is that broadcast joins are not suitable for every join scenario, and there is no set limit on DataFrame size so as to define the smaller DataFrame. But as a best practice, DataFrames sized between 10 MB and 50 MB are usually broadcast. Spark also performs broadcast joins implicitly. This behavior is controlled with the help of the Spark configuration, `spark.sql.autoBroadcastJoinThreshold`. The default threshold is 10 MB for the configuration. To disable the configuration, we can set it to `-1`.

Next, we will learn about Apache Arrow in Pandas.

Learning about Apache Arrow in Pandas

Apache Arrow is an in-memory columnar data format that helps to efficiently store data between clustered **Java Virtual Machines** (**JVMs**) and Python processes. This is highly beneficial for data scientists working with Pandas and **NumPy** in Databricks. Apache Arrow does not produce different results in terms of the data. It is helpful when we are converting Spark DataFrames to Pandas DataFrames, and vice versa. Let's try to better understand the utility of Apache Arrow with an analogy.

Let's say you were traveling to Europe before the establishment of the **European Union** (**EU**). To visit 10 countries in 7 days, you would have has to spend some time at every border for passport control, and money would have always been lost due to currency exchange. Similarly, without using Apache Arrow, inefficiencies exist due to serialization and deserialization processes wasting memory and CPU resources (such as converting a Spark DataFrame to a Pandas DataFrame).

But using Apache Arrow is like traveling to Europe after the establishment of the EU. This means no more waiting at the borders, and the same currency being used everywhere. Therefore, Apache Arrow allows us to use the same in-memory data format for different frameworks and file formats. This highly optimizes data conversions between Spark and Pandas. In Databricks, Apache Arrow is available as an optimization when converting a **PySpark** DataFrame to a Pandas DataFrame with the `toPandas()` function, and when converting a Pandas DataFrame to a PySpark DataFrame using the `createDataFrame()` function:

1. In order to enable Apache Arrow in Databricks, we need to enable the following Spark configuration:

```
spark.conf.set("spark.sql.execution.arrow.enabled",
"true")
```

2. We will now go through a quick example to understand how to enable and use Apache Arrow in Databricks. The following code block imports the Pandas and NumPy packages and enables Apache Arrow:

```
import numpy as np
import pandas as pd
spark.conf.set("spark.sql.execution.arrow.enabled",
"true")
```

3. Next, we can create a Pandas DataFrame using the following code:

```
pdf = pd.DataFrame(np.random.rand(1000, 3))
```

4. Now, we will create a Spark DataFrame from the Pandas DataFrame and display it using the following code block:

```
df = spark.createDataFrame(pdf)
display(df)
```

A point to note here is that even though we are enabling Apache Arrow, working with Pandas still leads to data getting collected on the driver node using the `toPandas()` function. Therefore, it should only be used on a small subset of data.

In the next section, we will learn about shuffle partitions in Spark and how to optimize them.

Understanding shuffle partitions

Every time Spark performs a wide transformation or aggregations, shuffling of data across the nodes occurs. And during these shuffle operations, Spark, by default, changes the partitions of the DataFrame. For example, when creating a DataFrame, it may have 10 partitions, but as soon as the shuffle occurs, Spark may change the partitions of the DataFrame to 200. These are what we call the shuffle partitions.

This is a default behavior in Spark, but it can be altered to improve the performance of Spark jobs. We can also confirm the default behavior by running the following line of code:

```
spark.conf.get('spark.sql.shuffle.partitions')
```

This returns the output of 200. This means that Spark will change the shuffle partitions to 200 by default. To alter this configuration, we can run the following code, which configures the shuffle partitions to 8:

```
spark.conf.set('spark.sql.shuffle.partitions',8)
```

You may be wondering why we set the spark.sql.shuffle.partitions configuration to 8. This is because we have eight cores in the cluster we are using. And having the same number of shuffle partitions ensures that during the shuffling process, we will have all the cores' clusters processing the same number of partitions at a time.

Next, we will be learning about caching in Spark.

Understanding caching in Spark

Every time we perform an action on a Spark DataFrame, Spark has to re-read the data from the source, run jobs, and provide an output as the result. This may not be a performance bottleneck when reading data for the first time, but if a certain DataFrame needs to be queried repeatedly, Spark will have to re-compute it every time. In such scenarios, Spark caching proves to be highly useful. Spark *caching* means that we store data in the cluster's memory. As we already know, Spark has memory divided for cached DataFrames and performing operations. Every time a DataFrame is cached in memory, it is stored in the cluster's memory, and Spark does not have to re-read it from the source in order to perform computations on the same DataFrame.

> **Note**
> Spark caching is a transformation and therefore it is evaluated *lazily*. In order to enforce a cache on a DataFrame, we need to call an *action*.

Now, you may be wondering how this is different from **Delta caching**, which we discussed in *Chapter 6, Databricks Delta Lake*. The following table illustrates the differences between Delta caching and Spark caching:

Feature	Delta Caching	Spark Caching
Storage	In the local storage of worker nodes	In memory blocks of the cluster
Applied to	Any Delta or Parquet table on Azure Data Lake, Azure Blob Storage, or another filesystem	Any DataFrame or Resilient Distributed Dataset

Feature	Delta Caching	Spark Caching
Triggered	Automatically trigger if Delta caching is enabled	Needs to be triggered manually
Evaluated	Lazy evaluation	Lazy evaluation
Force cache	Using the CACHE and SELECT statements	Using .cache and an action to materialize the cache
Availability	Can be enabled or disabled (not available on certain node types)	Always available

Figure 7.2 – Differences between Delta caching and Spark caching

Another point to note is that when a Databricks cluster is terminated, the cache is also lost. Now, we will go through a worked-out example to better understand Spark caching in Databricks:

1. We will start by creating a Spark DataFrame. First, we will define the schema manually for creating the DataFrame. Run the following code block:

```python
from pyspark.sql.types import *
from pyspark.sql.functions import *
manual_schema = StructType([
  StructField('Year',IntegerType(),True),
  StructField('Month',IntegerType(),True),
  StructField('DayofMonth',IntegerType(),True),
  StructField('DayOfWeek',IntegerType(),True),
  StructField('DepTime',StringType(),True),
  StructField('CRSDepTime',IntegerType(),True),
  StructField('ArrTime',StringType(),True),
  StructField('CRSArrTime',IntegerType(),True),
  StructField('UniqueCarrier',StringType(),True),
  StructField('FlightNum',IntegerType(),True),
  StructField('TailNum',StringType(),True),
  StructField('ActualElapsedTime',StringType(),True),
```

We will let you take the remaining code from the GitHub repository:

```
https://github.com/PacktPublishing/Optimizing-Databricks-
Workload
```

2. Now, we will create the airlines DataFrame that we have been using throughout the book. Run the following code block to create a Spark DataFrame:

```
airlines_1987_to_2008 = (
  spark
  .read
  .option("header",True)
  .option("delimiter",",")
  .schema(manual_schema)
  .csv("dbfs:/databricks-datasets/asa/airlines/*")
)
```

3. Next, we will run an aggregation query on the DataFrame. Here, we are grouping by the Year column and returning the number of records by the year. Note the time taken for the query to run:

```
display(airlines_1987_to_2008
         .groupBy(col("Year"))
         .count()
         .orderBy(col('count').desc())
        )
```

The query took *1.10 minutes* to run. Please note that it can take a few minutes to execute. Next, we will cache the DataFrame and then re-run the query.

4. To cache the DataFrame, run the following code. The syntax is <dataframe>. cache(). Here, we are calling an action immediately after the cache() function. This is done to materialize the cache:

```
airlines_1987_to_2008.cache().count()
```

Since the DataFrame has more than 100 million records, we can expect the code to execute in a few minutes. As soon as the code has executed, we can re-run the aggregation query.

5. Run the following code block to re-run the aggregation query on the DataFrame. Note the time taken for the query to run:

```
display(airlines_1987_to_2008
    .groupBy(col("Year"))
    .count()
    .orderBy(col('count').desc())
)
```

This time, the query took only *2.08 seconds*! And that is the power of Spark caching.

6. To further validate the cache, we can head over to the Spark UI and click on the **Storage** section. Here, we can find the details of the DataFrame that has been recently cached. The following screenshot shows the DataFrame that has been cached and other related details:

Storage Level	Cached Partitions	Fraction Cached	Size in Memory	Size on Disk
Disk Memory Deserialized 1x Replicated	93	100%	3.4 GiB	0.0 B

Figure 7.3 – Cached DataFrame details

The preceding screenshot confirms that all 93 partitions of the `airlines_1987_to_2008` DataFrame have been cached, and its size in memory is 3.4 GiB.

7. To remove a DataFrame from the cache, we can run the following code:

```
airlines_1987_to_2008.unpersist()
```

The `unpersist()` function is used to un-cache a DataFrame.

This concludes our section on Spark caching. Next, we will learn about AQE in Databricks.

Learning about AQE

We already know how Spark works under the hood. Whenever we execute transformations, Spark prepares a plan, and as soon as an action is called, it performs those transformations. Now, it's time to expand that knowledge. Let's dive deeper into Spark's query execution mechanism.

Every time a query is executed by Spark, it is done with the help of the following four plans:

- **Parsed Logical Plan**: Spark prepares a *Parsed Logical Plan*, where it checks the metadata (table name, column names, and more) to confirm whether the respective entities exist or not.

- **Analyzed Logical Plan**: Spark accepts the Parsed Logical Plan and converts it into what is called the *Analyzed Logical Plan*. This is then sent to Spark's catalyst optimizer, which is an advanced query optimizer for Spark.

- **Optimized Logical Plan**: The catalyst optimizer applies further optimizations and comes up with the final logical plan, called the *Optimized Logical Plan*.

- **Physical Plan**: The *Physical Plan* specifies how the Optimized Logical Plan is going to be executed on the cluster.

Apart from the catalyst optimizer, there is another framework in Spark called the **cost-based optimizer** (**CBO**). The CBO collects statistics on data, such as the number of distinct values, row counts, null values, and more, to help Spark come up with a better Physical Plan. AQE is another optimization technique that speeds up query execution based on runtime statistics. It does this with the help of the following three features:

- **Dynamically coalescing shuffle partitions**
- **Dynamically switching join strategies**
- **Dynamically optimizing skew joins**

Let's discuss these in detail.

Dynamically coalescing shuffle partitions

When dealing with very large datasets, shuffle has a huge impact on performance. It is an expensive operation that requires data to be moved across nodes so that it can be re-distributed as required by the downstream operations. But two types of issues can occur:

- If the number of partitions is less, then their size will be larger, and this can lead to data spillage during the shuffle. This can slow down Spark jobs.

- If the number of partitions is more, then there could be a chance that the partitions would be small in size, leading to a greater number of tasks. This can put more burden on Spark's task scheduler.

To solve these problems, we can set a relatively large number of shuffle partitions and then coalesce any adjacent small partitions at runtime. This can be achieved with the help of AQE, as it automatically coalesces small partitions at runtime.

Dynamically switching join strategies

With the help of AQE, Spark can switch join strategies at runtime if they are found to be inefficient. Spark supports various join strategies but usually, the *broadcast hash join* (also called the *broadcast join*) is often considered to be the most performant if one side of the join is small enough to fit in the memory of every node.

Dynamically optimizing skew joins

Data skew occurs when data is unevenly distributed across the partitions of the DataFrame. It has the potential to downgrade query performance. With the help of AQE, Spark can automatically detect data skew while joins are created. After detection, it splits the larger of those partitions into smaller sub-partitions that are joined to the corresponding partition on the other side of the join. This ensures that the Spark job does not get stuck due to a single enormously large partition.

Now, let's go through a worked-out example to learn how AQE actually works in Databricks:

1. First, we need to ensure that AQE is enabled. In Databricks Runtime 8.3, it is enabled by default. To enable it manually, we can run the following code:

```
spark.conf.set('spark.sql.adaptive.enabled','true')
```

2. Next, we will create an `items` Delta table that will contain two columns: `item_sku` and `price`. Run the following code to create the table:

```
%sql
-- Create "items" table.
CREATE TABLE items
USING delta
AS
SELECT id AS item_sku,
CAST(rand() * 1000 AS INT) AS price
FROM RANGE(30000000);
```

3. Now, we will create another Delta table called `sales`. This table will contain three columns, `item_sku`, `quantity`, and `date`. We will later join the `sales` table with the `items` table. The `sales` table simply represents the items from the `items` table that were sold on the respective date. We are purposely creating this table in a skewed fashion where the item with an `item_sku` value of `200` is in nearly 80% of all the sales. Run the following code to create the table:

```sql
%sql
-- Create "sales" table with skew.
-- Item with id 200 is in 80% of all sales.
CREATE TABLE sales
USING delta
AS
SELECT CASE WHEN rand() < 0.8 THEN 200 ELSE CAST(rand() *
30000000 AS INT) END AS item_sku,
CAST(rand() * 100 AS INT) AS quantity,
DATE_ADD(current_date(), - CAST(rand() * 360 AS INT)) AS
date
FROM RANGE(1000000000);
```

4. We can get a glimpse of the data in the two tables by running the following queries. Run the following code to query the `items` table:

```sql
%sql SELECT * FROM items
```

5. Run the following code to query the `sales` table:

```sql
%sql SELECT * FROM sales
```

6. Next, we will run a query to observe the dynamic coalescing of shuffle partitions with AQE. Let's run an aggregation query:

```sql
%sql
SELECT date, sum(quantity) AS total_quantity
FROM sales
GROUP BY date
ORDER BY total_quantity DESC;
```

Here, we are trying to query the total sales grouped by date. Next, we can open the **Associated SQL Query** diagram of the query in the Spark UI. You can find this option in the **SQL** section of the Spark UI. If we expand the **Exchange** box, we can see that the partitions after aggregation are very small in size (roughly 13 KB on average):

Exchange +details

Stages: 57.0

shuffle records written	6,480
shuffle write time total (min, med, max)	478 ms (18 ms, 22 ms, 55 ms)
records read	6,480
local bytes read	102.8 KiB
fetch wait time	0 ms
remote bytes read	128.9 KiB
local blocks read	8
remote blocks read	10
data size total (min, med, max)	151.9 KiB (8.4 KiB, 8.4 KiB, 8.4 KiB)
remote bytes read to disk	0.0 B
shuffle bytes written total (min, med, max)	231.7 KiB (12.7 KiB, 12.9 KiB, 12.9 KiB)

Figure 7.4 – The Exchange box in the Associated SQL Query diagram

AQE automatically identified the small partitions and has coalesced those numerous small partitions into one large partition. This is confirmed by the **CustomShuffleReader** box. In the following screenshot, we can see that the number of partitions equals 1. This is the result of coalescing several small partitions into one single partition so that we have only one task and therefore a lower load on Spark's task scheduler.

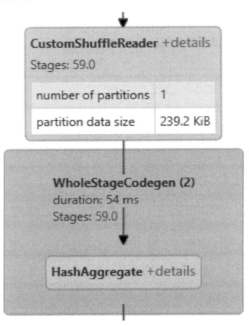

Figure 7.5 – The CustomShuffleReader box in the Associated SQL Query diagram

7. Next, we will run a query to observe dynamically switching join strategies. We will run a query that returns the total sales amount, grouped by date, for items with a price lower than 10. Before we execute the query, let's take a look at the query's Physical Plan:

```
%sql
EXPLAIN FORMATTED
SELECT date, sum(quantity * price) AS total_sales
FROM sales AS s
JOIN items AS i ON s.item_sku = i.item_sku
WHERE price < 10
GROUP BY date
ORDER BY total_sales DESC;
```

We can clearly note in the Physical Plan that Spark intends to perform a *sort-merge join*. In this kind of join strategy, Spark sorts both the datasets and then performs an inner join between them. It is considered to be a computationally expensive join operation.

8. Let's execute the query with AQE enabled. Run the following code block:

```sql
%sql
SELECT date, sum(quantity * price) AS total_sales
FROM sales AS s
JOIN items AS i ON s.item_sku = i.item_sku
WHERE price < 10
GROUP BY date
ORDER BY total_sales DESC;
```

9. Let's take a look at the executed query's **Associated SQL Query** diagram in the Spark UI. We can clearly see that Spark has changed the join strategy at runtime. From a sort-merge join, it has dynamically switched to a broadcast hash join.

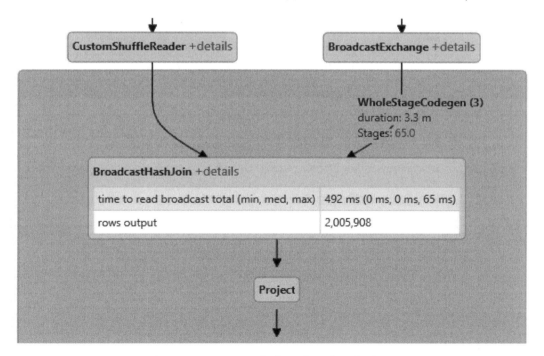

Figure 7.6 – The join strategy switched to a broadcast hash join at runtime

10. Next, we will look at how Spark dynamically optimizes skew joins with the help of AQE. To do this, let's execute the following query:

```sql
%sql
SELECT date, sum(quantity * price) AS total_sales
FROM sales AS s
JOIN items AS i ON s.item_sku = i.item_sku
GROUP BY date
ORDER BY total_sales DESC;
```

Here, we are trying to query the total sales grouped by date.

11. Now, let's check the **Associated SQL Query** diagram of the query in the Spark UI. This will help us understand exactly what happened under the hood:

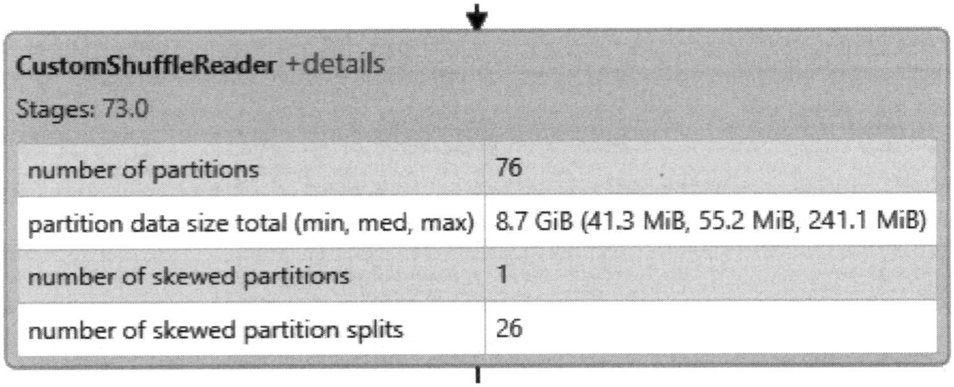

CustomShuffleReader +details

Stages: 73.0

number of partitions	76
partition data size total (min, med, max)	8.7 GiB (41.3 MiB, 55.2 MiB, 241.1 MiB)
number of skewed partitions	1
number of skewed partition splits	26

Figure 7.7 – Number of skewed partitions and splits

Here, we can see that one partition is skewed (the item with an `item_sku` value of `200`) in the **CustomShuffleReader** box. This single skewed partition is further split into `26` different partitions, due to AQE.

This brings us to the end of the section on AQE. As we can see, AQE is a highly beneficial Spark optimization technique that helps to speed up queries at query runtime. And in most of the latest **Databricks Runtime** (**DBR**) versions, it comes enabled by default.

Summary

In this chapter, we learned about several optimization techniques concerning Spark Core. We started off by learning about broadcast joins and how they are more performant than a standard join. Then, we learned about the advantages of using Apache Arrow with Pandas. Next, we learned about shuffle partitions and Spark caching.

Finally, we learned about AQE and how it helps to speed up queries during runtime. All these optimization techniques are highly useful for tuning big data workloads in Azure Databricks.

In the next chapter, we will learn about real-world case studies with Databricks. We will learn about modern-day solution architectures using Azure Databricks across different industries and sectors.

Section 3: Real-World Scenarios

In this section, we learn from real-world examples how Databricks is helping organizations build massive-scale data engineering and data science applications.

This section comprises the following chapter:

- *Chapter 8, Case Studies*

8
Case Studies

Data teams across the world are using Databricks to solve the toughest data problems. Every Databricks success story brings a unique set of challenges and new learning for architects and data professionals. Databricks can be used as a transformation layer, a real-time streaming engine, or a solution for machine learning and advanced analytics. In this chapter, we will look at several real-world case study examples and learn how Databricks is used to help drive innovation across various industries around the world.

In this chapter, we will learn about use cases from the following industries:

- Learning case studies from the manufacturing industry
- Learning case studies from the media and entertainment industry
- Learning case studies from the retail and FMCG industry
- Learning case studies from the pharmaceutical industry
- Learning case studies from the e-commerce industry
- Learning case studies from the logistics and supply chain industry

Let's begin with the case studies from the manufacturing industry.

Learning case studies from the manufacturing industry

Data and statistical analysis help manufacturing organizations make accurate decisions and streamline processes. This makes manufacturing processes become more efficient and prevents unwanted losses for the organizations.

Case study 1 – leading automobile manufacturing company

An organization was looking for a cloud-scale analytics platform to support growing **online analytical processing** (**OLAP**) requirements, a modernized visualization capability to support business intelligence needs, and advanced analytical and **artificial intelligence** (**AI**) solutions for existing data.

The proposed solution architecture was as follows:

- Data from the Oracle database and flat files was extracted using Azure Data Factory and loaded into Azure Data Lake.
- Azure Databricks was used to transform the historical data. Then, the data would be loaded into the Azure Synapse Data Warehouse.
- A lead scoring system was built using Azure Databricks for predictive analytics.
- Data modeling was performed in Power BI, and several reports and dashboards were built using the historical and predicted data.

The solution architecture is depicted in the following diagram:

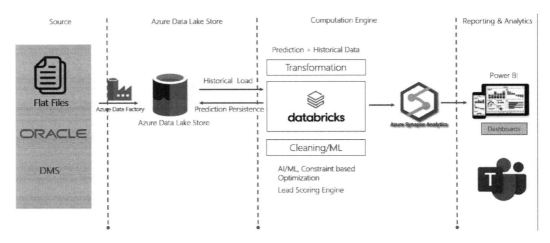

Figure 8.1 – Solution architecture diagram for the leading automobile manufacturing company

Next, we will learn about another automobile manufacturing case study.

Case study 2 – international automobile manufacturing giant

A automobile manufacturing giant faced several challenges in its data journey. They were previously using an on-premises SQL Server that had performance limitations, leading to access to refreshed data being reduced. Other significant issues that were faced by the organization included scalability issues, the absence of real-time data analytics, lower utilization of Power BI premium features, and limited self-service analytics. The proposed solution architecture was as follows:

- Data from Microsoft Dynamics 365 and the on-premises database was pushed to Azure Data Lake.

- Azure Databricks was used for parallel and in-memory data cleaning and massaging.

- A data model was built using **Azure Synapse Analytics**, thereby helping to access data with minimal data preparation activities and an efficient mechanism to manage large volumes of data.

- Power BI reports and dashboards were built on top of the data in Azure Synapse Analytics.

The solution architecture is depicted in the following diagram:

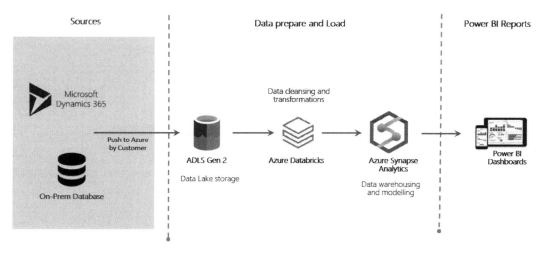

Figure 8.2 – Solution architecture diagram for the international automobile manufacturing giant

Next, we will learn about a chemical corporate case study.

Case study 3 – graph search in a chemical corporate firm

A chemical corporate firm was having an issue with the chemical composition of mixtures and products and their test results. They were also struggling with the sales data of a particular chemical. The scenario was focused on querying data and information for a UK-based firm that stores production data in various stages and forms that have complex parent-child relationships. The major task was to create metadata and relationships in the data so that it could be queried using a graph database, without utilizing much of its compute power, as well within the time constraint of 5 seconds. The proposed solution architecture was as follows:

- The data from CSV files and the real-time feed from Azure Event Hubs were imported, cleaned, and transformed using Azure Databricks.

- After forming relationships and transforming data into graphs in Azure Databricks, data was pushed into Azure Cosmos DB.

- The data was queried using the Gremlin API of Azure Cosmos Graph and questions such as "*In the last 3 years, who did we sell materials to and in what quantity?*" and "*What products contain chemical X or its derived chemical and in what quantity?*" were answered.

- Power BI was used to visualize this real-time streaming data for recording and information scoring purposes.

The solution architecture is depicted in the following diagram:

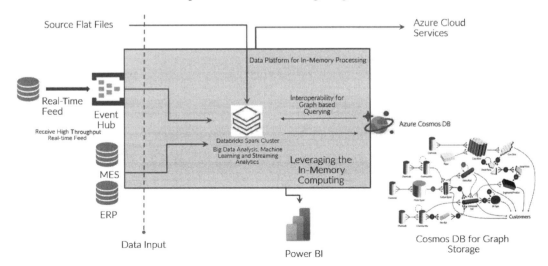

Figure 8.3 – Solution architecture diagram for the chemical corporate firm

Next, we will learn about a case study from a leading medical equipment manufacturer.

Case study 4 – real-time loyalty engine for a leading medical equipment manufacturer

This case study is about capturing customer behaviors and calculating loyalty points and tiers for a customer in near-real time. There were about five different sources of data where these behaviors were tracked that needed to be pulled into **Azure Data Lake** in real time, calculations done and stored (history tracking enabled), and then the calculated information (summary and details) was passed to a data hub (Cosmos DB) that would eventually be consumed by the presentation layer.

The idea was to deliver this on the Azure platform with Azure Databricks being the real-time processing engine. Currently, the engine is live with one source of behavior – that is, *Salesforce* – where the real-time orders get processed based on the rule criteria where the points are allocated. The engine is highly configurable, which means that adding a new source, rule, or behavior will not affect the code or need any code changes. The in-memory rule parser was designed to parse any rule criteria over the incoming data efficiently.

The solution architecture is depicted in the following diagram:

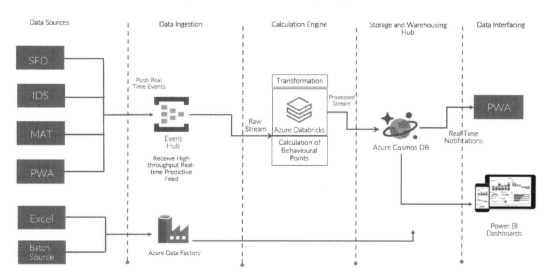

Figure 8.4 – Solution architecture diagram for the leading medical equipment manufacturer

Next, we will learn about a case study from the media and entertainment industry.

Learning case studies from the media and entertainment industry

Data plays a crucial role for media and entertainment organizations as it helps them understand viewer behavior and identify the true market value of the content being shared. This helps in improving the quality of content being delivered and at the same time opens up new monetization avenues for the production houses.

Case study 5 – HD Insights to Databricks migration for a media giant

In this case study, the prime requirement of the organization was processing and number crunching datasets that were 2-3 TB in size every day. This was required to perform analytics on on-demand advertising video service's user data to generate reports and dashboards for the marketing team. Also, the organization was not able to automate the **extract, transform, and load** (**ETL**) process of their web and mobile platform viewer's data. This ETL process was being executed using Azure HD Insights. Moreover, managing HD Insights was an operational overhead. Besides this, they were also interested in performance and cost optimization for their ETL jobs.

Migrating ETL workloads from HD Insights to Azure Databricks helped reduce costs by 26%. Azure Databricks, being a fully managed service, eliminated the operational overhead of managing the platform, therefore increasing productivity. Databricks' seamless integration with the Azure ecosystem helped in automating the processes using Azure Data Factory.

Caching data within Delta Lake helped to provide the much-needed acceleration of queries. Also, managing Spark clusters with auto-scaling and decoupling compute and storage helped to simplify the organization's infrastructure and further optimize operational costs. The migration from Hadoop to Databricks delivered significant value by reducing the cost of failure, increasing processing speeds, and simplifying data exploration for ad hoc analytics.

The complete customer success story can be read here: `https://databricks.com/customers/viacom18`. The solution architecture is depicted in the following diagram:

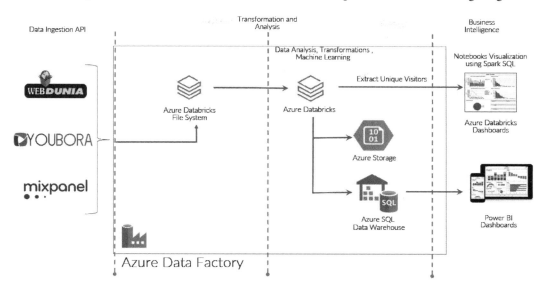

Figure 8.5 – Solution architecture diagram for the media giant

Next, we will learn about a case study from the retail and FMCG industry.

Learning case studies from the retail and FMCG industry

Data is more important than ever for the retail and FMCG industry. It can be very helpful for maintaining a lean inventory. In addition, data is critical for optimizing the prices of products on demand. Also, a data-driven approach can boost relationships with business partners, thereby helping to smoothen the supply chain.

Case study 6 – real-time analytics using IoT Hub for a retail giant

An organization wanted to build an end-to-end solution wherein edge devices gathered metrics at a certain frequency from all the instruments on the floor shop. These metrics were to be utilized to conduct edge analytics for real-time issues. Thereon, the data would be pushed to a cloud platform where near-real-time data transformations would be done and delivered to a dashboard for visualization. The same data would be persisted for batch processing and leveraged machine learning to gain insights.

The proposed solution architecture was as follows:

- Three devices (three metrics per device) were integrated with Azure **IoT Hub** to get the real-time device telemetry data into the Azure cloud.

- From IoT Hub, the data points were consumed by Azure Databricks to perform real-time transformation and to prepare useful insights.

- The transformed data was pushed to Power BI for live dashboard generation and to enable attentiveness when the data changed beyond the configured limits (Alert Mechanism).

The solution architecture is depicted in the following diagram:

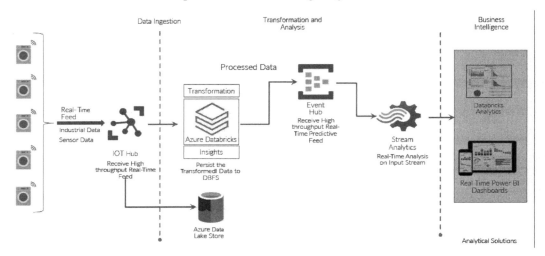

Figure 8.6 – Solution architecture diagram for the retail giant

Next, we will learn about a case study from the pharmaceutical industry.

Learning case studies from the pharmaceutical industry

Data analytics and AI in the pharmaceutical industry play a crucial role in optimizing clinical trials, analyzing patients' behavior, improving logistics, and reducing costs.

Case study 7 – pricing analytics for a pharmaceutical company

The organization required a pricing decision support framework to get insights on gross margin increment based on historical events, the prioritization of SKUs, review indicators, and more. The framework was to be designed in a way so that the smart machine learning models could be transferred and scaled to retain the quality and depth of the information gathered.

A pricing decision framework was developed using machine learning on Azure Databricks, which helped to predict the SKU that should go for pricing review. The system was also capable of predicting the next month's volume, which helped in deciding the correct price for a specific SKU.

The solution architecture is depicted in the following diagram:

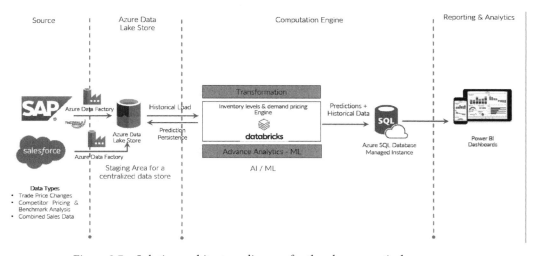

Figure 8.7 – Solution architecture diagram for the pharmaceutical company

Next, we will learn about a case study from the e-commerce industry.

Learning case studies from the e-commerce industry

Big data analytics in the e-commerce industry helps businesses understand consumer purchase patterns, improve user experience, and increase revenue.

Case study 8 – migrating interactive analytical apps from Redshift to Postgres

An organization in the e-commerce space was using AWS Redshift as their data warehouse and Databricks as their ETL engine. The setup was deployed across different data centers in different regions on **Amazon Web Services** (**AWS**) and **Google Cloud Platform** (**GCP**). They were also running into performance bottlenecks and were incurring egress costs unnecessarily. The data was growing faster than the compute required to process that data. AWS Redshift was unable to independently scale storage and compute. Hence, the organization decided to migrate its data and analytics landscape to Azure.

AWS Redshift's data was migrated to Azure Database for PostgreSQL Hyperscale (Citus). Citus is an open source extension to Postgres. It transforms Postgres into a distributed database where data can be sharded or partitioned across multiple nodes of the server. The migration effort was minimal as Redshift is also based on PostgreSQL. It took about 2 weeks to migrate from Redshift to Hyperscale (Citus). The highlights of the migration were as follows:

- 600 tables were migrated. Over 500 of them were distributed across the worker nodes of Postgres Hyperscale (Citus).

- Nearly 80% of the queries were dropped in, with no modifications.

- Almost 200 Databricks jobs were dropped in, with minimal changes. This is because Redshift uses the same JDBC driver that Azure Database does for PostgreSQL Hyperscale (Citus).

The complete customer success story can be read here: `https://techcommunity.microsoft.com/t5/azure-database-for-postgresql/migrating-interactive-analytics-apps-from-redshift-to-postgres/ba-p/1825730`. The solution architecture is depicted in the following diagram:

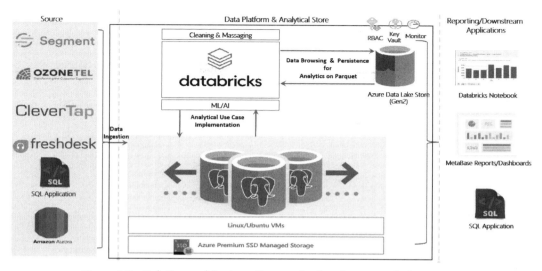

Figure 8.8 – Solution architecture diagram for the pharmaceutical company

Next, we will learn about a case study from the logistics and supply chain industry.

Learning case studies from the logistics and supply chain industry

Data analytics and machine learning play a crucial role in the functioning of the logistics and supply chain industry. Data can help reduce inefficiencies in the supply chain processes and optimize deliveries at the same time. Machine learning and predictive analytics help in better planning, procurement, and consumer fulfillment.

Case study 9 – accelerating intelligent insights with tailored big data analytics

An organization wanted to create an end-to-end data warehousing platform on Azure. Their original process involved manually collecting data from siloed sources and creating necessary reports from it. There was a need to integrate all the data sources and implement a single source of truth, which would be on the Azure cloud. The proposed solution architecture was as follows:

- Full load and incremental data pipelines were developed using Azure Data Factory to ingest data into Azure Synapse (data warehouse). Azure Synapse also allows you to build pipelines, just like Azure Data Factory. Refer to the following link for differences between the two: `https://docs.microsoft.com/en-us/azure/synapse-analytics/data-integration/concepts-data-factory-differences`.

- Data was loaded in **Azure Data Lake Storage** (**ADLS**) for big data transformations and analytics in Azure Databricks.

- The data lake was mounted on Azure Databricks for complex transformations and advanced use cases such as machine learning.

- The modeling that was done on the synapse layer included creating optimized views and tables that implemented business logic.

- Data modeling on Azure Analysis Services included defining relationships and creating the columns, measures, and tables necessary for Power BI's **key performance indicators** (**KPIs**).

- Cubes were created on Azure Analysis Services to ensure that data was refreshed quicker for Power BI reports. The reports were also created for a multi-lingual interface.

The solution architecture is depicted in the following diagram:

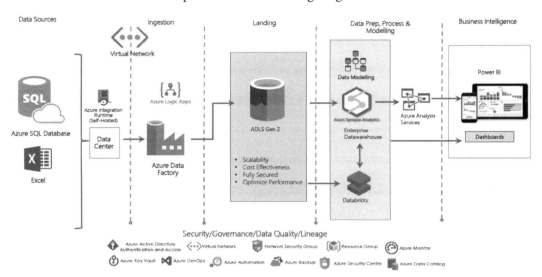

Figure 8.9 – Solution architecture diagram for the logistics and supply chain company

This brings us to the end of the case studies. To learn about more Databricks success stories, check out the official page: `https://databricks.com/customers`.

Summary

In this chapter, we learned about several Databricks case studies, ranging from manufacturing and media to logistics and the supply chain. All these solution architectures have employed Databricks in different ways. Irrespective of its role in an organization's data journey, Databricks has always emerged as a game-changer in the world of big data analytics.

This brings us to the end of this book. We learned quite a lot about Spark and Databricks, starting with the fundamentals and quickly moving toward optimization techniques and best practices. We learned about how Delta Lake, MLflow, and Koalas help make Databricks a complete and cloud-first data platform for all data engineering and data science needs.

`Packt.com`

Subscribe to our online digital library for full access to over 7,000 books and videos, as well as industry leading tools to help you plan your personal development and advance your career. For more information, please visit our website.

Why subscribe?

- Spend less time learning and more time coding with practical eBooks and Videos from over 4,000 industry professionals

- Improve your learning with Skill Plans built especially for you

- Get a free eBook or video every month

- Fully searchable for easy access to vital information

- Copy and paste, print, and bookmark content

Did you know that Packt offers eBook versions of every book published, with PDF and ePub files available? You can upgrade to the eBook version at `packt.com` and as a print book customer, you are entitled to a discount on the eBook copy. Get in touch with us at `customercare@packtpub.com` for more details.

At `www.packt.com`, you can also read a collection of free technical articles, sign up for a range of free newsletters, and receive exclusive discounts and offers on Packt books and eBooks.

Other Books You May Enjoy

If you enjoyed this book, you may be interested in these other books by Packt:

Azure Databricks Cookbook

Phani Raj, Vinod Jaiswal

ISBN: 978-1-78980-971-8

- Read and write data from and to various Azure resources and file formats
- Build a modern data warehouse with Delta Tables and Azure Synapse Analytics
- Explore jobs, stages, and tasks and see how Spark lazy evaluation works
- Handle concurrent transactions and learn performance optimization in Delta tables
- Learn Databricks SQL and create real-time dashboards in Databricks SQL
- Integrate Azure DevOps for version control, deploying, and productionizing solutions with CI/CD pipelines
- Discover how to use RBAC and ACLs to restrict data access
- Build end-to-end data processing pipeline for near real-time data analytics

Distributed Data Systems with Azure Databricks

Alan Bernardo Palacio

ISBN: 978-1-83864-721-6

- Create ETLs for big data in Azure Databricks
- Train, manage, and deploy machine learning and deep learning models
- Integrate Databricks with Azure Data Factory for extract, transform, load (ETL) pipeline creation
- Discover how to use Horovod for distributed deep learning
- Find out how to use Delta Engine to query and process data from Delta Lake
- Understand how to use Data Factory in combination with Databricks
- Use Structured Streaming in a production-like environment

Packt is searching for authors like you

If you're interested in becoming an author for Packt, please visit `authors.packtpub.com` and apply today. We have worked with thousands of developers and tech professionals, just like you, to help them share their insight with the global tech community. You can make a general application, apply for a specific hot topic that we are recruiting an author for, or submit your own idea.

Share Your Thoughts

Now you've finished *Optimizing Databricks Workloads*, we'd love to hear your thoughts! Scan the QR code below to go straight to the Amazon review page for this book and share your feedback or leave a review on the site that you purchased it from.

https://packt.link/r/1-801-81907-6

Your review is important to us and the tech community and will help us make sure we're delivering excellent quality content.

Index

Symbols

A